After the Cold War and the Gulf War:

A NEW MOMENT IN AMERICA?

After the Cold War and the Gulf War:

A NEW MOMENT IN AMERICA?

Freedom House

Contents

Preface

This short book is the record of an unusual gathering of some 150 people that took place in Washington, D.C. on May 10 and 11 of 1991.

The speakers and participants at this gathering represented a variety of viewpoints and constituencies: labor and business, Democrats and Republicans, and the rest. But, more significantly, many came out of the trenches from the different sides of some of the most fiercely fought debates on foreign affairs and social policy of recent times. As *The Washington Post's* E.J. Dionne said during the meeting (with only a trace of exaggeration), it would have been difficult to have gotten this group together in the same room from 1972 until today.

The transcripts of public meetings do not always make good reading. Many of those involved in this meeting urged us to publish this one because they insisted it would prove an exception to that rule. They also felt this discussion would have interest beyond the particular communities from which our participants were drawn. We hope our hurried editing has enhanced, not weakened, its appeal.

The value of this discussion arises from the singularly high quality of the speakers' presentations. While they were all impressive, I believe other speakers would join me in paying special thanks to Congressman Stephen Solarz and Assistant Secretary of State Bernard Aronson for taking time out from the press of official duties to prepare such thoughtful presentations, and to Charles Krauthammer for his truly masterful keynote address.

Many individuals contributed generously of their time and talents to make our meeting possible, and to allow the prompt publication of this transcript. We are especially indebted to Charles Brown, Mike Chapman, Naomi Munson, Eric Singer and Victoria Thomas for assistance with editing, designing and proofreading this publication.

This transcript is based upon audio tapes made during the discussion. The speakers' remarks have been edited lightly to enhance clarity and readability. Some small gaps in the tapes were, however, unavoidable, and some words and phrases may have been misunderstood by those preparing the transcript. The transcript could not be reviewed before the publication date by all the participants, and should not, therefore, be viewed as a facsimile record of the event.

We are grateful to The Bayard Rustin Fund for a grant to cover the costs of the meeting facilities and meals. No fees or honoraria were paid to speakers, and virtually all speakers and participants paid their own costs of travel and accomodations. This itself, as Sam Leiken remarked, is evidence of a new moment.

I would also like to express my gratitude and satisfaction to colleagues who helped on the *ad hoc* committee that sponsored and organized this event: Rita Freedman, Robert Leiken, Sam Leiken and Bruce McColm. We are all grateful to Freedom House for facilitating the publication of this transcript, but we wish to make clear that the opinions reflected here represent those of the participants, not necessarily those of Freedom House itself.

-- Penn Kemble
May 27, 1991

Introduction

Penn Kemble

Penn Kemble is a Senior Associate at Freedom House, and a writer and television producer. He is a veteran of the civil rights movement and many political campaigns. He was one of the principal organizers of this conference; this introduction is adapted from his presentation to the opening dinner.

The organizers of this meeting were moved to convene it by two perceptions. One was that it might be valuable to discuss what could be done to assure that the democratic revolution that is now transforming the world can gain the greatest possible success. The other was our sense that, at the very time when so many in the world are embracing America's ideals, our own civic culture and morale suffer from listlessness, confusion, and divisions. Perhaps, some of us thought, not only can we do more to help the democratic revolution abroad; perhaps a closer engagement with the new democrats can help us strengthen our own public life.

Central and Eastern Europe have been the crucible in which, more than any other, this new moment has been shaped. Few of us were prepared for the vastness of the task of reconstruction these countries would face. In some measure, the surprise we find reflects the unwillingness so many in the

West had about acknowledging the realities of totalitarianism -- a word itself they found almost unbearable to pronounce. The work of reconstruction in the post-Communist world requires rebuilding from the bottom up: *Up From the Rubble*, in the title of Solzhenitsyn's book.

The transformation taking place in this region is an unusual one. Large, well-organized movements or parties have not overthrown an old order, as was the case in the French, Russian, and even American Revolutions. Under "really existing socialism," it was hard for a new society to develop inside the womb of the old (to borrow the Marxist phrase). There was simply no space for such development. Nevertheless, in the winter of 1989-1990, when the threat of armed repression in these societies suddenly and unexpectedly faltered, pro-Western and pro-democratic sentiments that had been building for years suddenly and spontaneously welled up. The old regimes were swept away. Communism simply collapsed.

But the creation of a new moral, political and legal authority to replace the old way of life is proving difficult and slow. It seems to require the almost complete demolition of what over there are called the "old structures." Today, even strategies of gradual change toward more democratic government, and of gently "sequencing" the transition to market economics, are proving untenable. Halfway measures simply do not work, and the only hope seems to be to press forward, despite the risks and hardships.

As they do press forward, the new democrats are learning something that may have some relevance for us here. Capitalism is what they want, and capitalism is what they need. But they can't count on the capitalists to solve all the problems. It seems that just as our left-wing intelligentsia proved naive about totalitarianism, so some anti-communists slipped into their own, more innocent naiveté about capitalism.

When I first visited Central Europe in the early 1980s I realized that there was often a kind of mirror-imaging in the minds of Communist-trained intellectuals. It persisted even after they made the break with Marxism-Leninism. They seemed to imagine that the capitalist world was an organized, politically purposive world system. They actually hoped that we were in fact what the KGB said we were, and that someday one of the tentacles of the capitalist monster would reach out to rescue them.

The truth has been disappointing. As the work of rebuilding post-Communist Europe goes forward, the capitalists are holding back, taking a wait-and-see attitude. Private investment in the region is lagging, and the money that is available comes mainly from Western governments, and from international financial institutions backed by governments. This has been a disappointment to some U.S. officials, who had hoped the private sector would carry more of the burden. It has also been a disappointment to some of the new democrats, who fear that they will be held accountable for encouraging expectations that cannot be met.

Evidently the "really existing capitalists" are aware that the free market system is not just a modular technology that can be plugged in where the old socialist economic machinery once stood. The capitalists understand that the free market system is not a natural, Garden-of-Eden state of human affairs. Before the market can function, there has to be some civil, social, and, ultimately, moral order. Private property rests on the existence of civil law and its enforcement. Capital investment and entrepreneurial development do not thrive under looming clouds of political disorder.

Capitalism requires some kind of social contract. And, in our times, the social contract that commands the most authority, and therefore the kind most beneficial to the capitalists, is the kind that rests upon the democratic consent of the governed.

There is, however, a strain in the left which imagines that some of the "old structures" of the socialist world can be adapted to work in harness with free enterprise. For them, the social market economy means "socialist market economy": one of those formulae in which three small letters make a world of difference. But it is becoming clear that these societies cannot rebuild so long as Communists or former Communists play a large role; no one wants them as partners to a social contract.

There is also a strain within the American right -- call it libertarian or *laissez faire* -- which imagines that the polity can only encumber or interfere with proper economic activities. Its maxim is, "That government is best which governs least."

In each its own way, these two antagonistic schools of thought have contributed to a tendency to underrate the importance of political and cultural factors in the reconstruction of post-Communist societies. They both have helped to foster an attitude that is something like what the Leninists used to call "economism." Even among staunch anti-Communists in our government and media, we find the idea that debt relief, currency stabilization, loans, credits, and a bit of technical advice are all that is necessary to send private entrepreneurs surging through Central Europe.

This economics-first approach is not frowned upon by some cynical elements on the left. They want the money to flow sooner, rather than later, so it can get over there while their old allies are still around to take advantage of it.

Americans, of course, do give some support to a variety of political and cultural development efforts in the region through the National Endowment for Democracy, AID, and some private foundations. We are helping to train parliamentarians and judges, to foster the independent media, to reform the educational curricula, to strengthen free trade unions, environmental watchdogs, political parties, and many other things.

But compared to the what we have spent on encouraging business development and on macro-economic stabilization, the amounts provided for these kinds of purposes have been small. More important -- because money may not be the most important measure of how we assist in the creation of a democratic polity and culture -- the *effort* we have made is small. Yet unless more rapid gains are made in strengthening the non-economic components of a free society, the money we are spending on the directly economic aspects may be wasted.

At the recent conference of the National Endowment for Democracy, a brilliant young Russian legal scholar, Oleg Rumyantsev, explained the problem of many of the emerging democracies this way:

> We have been abolishing many of the old practices, and creating many new institutions. Now we have to find out how these institutions can become rooted in the population.

What this means, one assumes, is that the peoples in the new democracies need to develop a clearer, stronger and more widely shared sense of democratic citizenship. It seems to some of us that this is a matter with which we in the United States might be more helpful. A question is, why haven't we?

One possible explanation is that the collapse of Communism and the rush of democratic spirit at the end, of the 1980s caught the West (and not least of all the United States, the world's chief bearer of the democratic idea) quite unprepared. I don't mean simply that it took us by surprise. I mean that our own culture was not exactly tingling with civic vitality at the time the East Germans began dancing on The Wall.

We ourselves are just emerging from a pervasive, generation-long conflict between our own New Left and New Right. The New Left born of the Sixties and Seventies certainly did not celebrate American democracy. It was not concerned about cultivating the virtues of democratic citizenship; it regarded those virtues as part of the yoke of oppression.

In response to the New Left, we got the New Right. The New Right brought into prominence some interesting groups and ideas. But it is unlikely that these forces would have gotten as far as they did if many other elements in the society had not gotten behind their candidate, Ronald Reagan, out of frustration over the effects of the left on the Democratic Party and the Carter Administration.

Although Ronald Reagan could be quite eloquent about democracy, by the time the people of Eastern Europe hit the streets, the Reagan era was drawing to a close. As the "Commentary" pages of *The Washington Times* remind us, today the American right does not present a very coherent view of America's role in the world, or a very clear idea about how a democratic society should order its affairs. The right is still sustaining itself -- and not badly, at that -- as the alternative to the left. But on both sides there is a gathering sense of exhaustion.

Perhaps this description of our own political temper is too negative. I am not arguing that American democracy is sick, or tottering. But remember E.M. Forster's World War II-era book, *Two Cheers for Democracy*? I recognize that enthusiasm of any kind has been in bad form recently. But one cheer seems to me to be about the present level of American support for democracy, as I read the applause meter. I can grant that three cheers may be a bit high. But wouldn't we be justified today in once again summoning up two fairly robust cheers for democracy?

Our left still belittles democracy: in the back of their minds, one suspects, it is still just bourgeois democracy, the guise for various oppressions. (This must be the distant ancestry of former President Carter's remarkable statement in Beijing, in which he praised the regime for the "respect" it shows its citizens by supposedly providing them with "a decent home, a job, and adequate health care.")

Our right has a very different problem: it sees democracy as a slippery slope, where one little misstep will send everything careening off to socialism, anarchy or whatever. Even after its populist successes with Ronald Reagan, Margaret Thatcher and Wenceslas Square, the Right is haunted by the Tory anxiety that the people will turn out to be a "great beast" that will devour the seed corn and trample the rights of property.

Has the persistence of this polarization in our own political argument somehow dulled our ability to respond to the remarkable democratic energies being released in Central and Eastern Europe, the Soviet Union, China, Latin America and Africa? Why have we responded to this astounding movement so half-heartedly?[1]

While money is surely needed by the new democracies, in the long run our contact, our encouragement, and our example may prove more important. *The New York Times* of May 1, 1991 carried a report on the kind of support I have in mind. An organization called Education for Democracy has recently sent several hundred American volunteers to Czechoslovakia to stay in the homes of families in outlying towns, where ordinary

---

[1] Shortly after this conference ended, a motion to cut the annual appropriation for our National Endowment for Democracy in half was defeated in the House of Representatives by a mere 35 votes. A majority of Democrats voted in favor of the cut. (Ed.)

citizens need conversation partners to learn English. These Americans pay most of their own costs, and work for subsistence wages.

In a conversation I had with Ann Gardner, the Executive Director of the group, she explained that their volunteers are besieged with all kinds of questions about how things are done in the United States. They often call or write back to get help on these matters from relatives and friends in the United States. This is an old tradition: the New England schoolmarm of the Reconstruction Era, the civil rights workers of the Sixties, the Peace Corps volunteers, the American kibbutzniks who spend a year or two in Israel.

I have no foolish illusion that activities such as this can, as a practical matter, carry the new democracies through the anxious and unpleasant transitions ahead. But I think that the *spirit* these kinds of activities embody could have very important effects.

Is it conceivable that pro-democracy groups and individuals in this country could come together to sponsor and encourage more citizen activities of this kind? Beyond this, could we provide a stronger network of support here for democrats who need help -- the Chinese students, the Russian democrats, the young Africans who recently spoke out so eloquently against the authoritarianism of their leaders? Could a network of democracy's friends here encourage initiatives by Congress or the Executive in support of the democratic cause abroad?

We are talking about a new moment in America, and speculation is encouraged. Those of us who organized this meeting discussed some possible benefits that closer contact with the new democrats might provide to our own politics and culture.

• The new democracies need to have both strong private sectors and strong governments. For some time, our political and economic debate here has been conducted as if one side of this equation could be strengthened only when the other is weakened. This could change. Pope John Paul II's recent encyclical, which addresses the challenges of post-Communist Europe, has this lesson for the left: "The free market is the most efficient instrument for utilizing resources and effectively responding to needs." But it also has this to say to the right: "There are collective and qualitative needs which cannot be satisfied by market mechanisms. There are important human needs which escape its logic."

- If the new democrats are going to succeed, they can have little patience with a mentality of victimhood or dependency. In their idea of citizenship, there will have to be firm responsibilities as well as rights. This too has obvious applications here in the U.S.

- Those citizens who benefit from the transition to democracy and the free market will also have responsibilities to meet. Rules will have to be respected, taxes will have to be paid. As economist Jeffrey Sachs has argued, the new structures of these societies can fall like a house of cards if those struggling at the bottom become convinced that others are reaping unjustifiably huge benefits through favoritism, corruption, or other means.

- Many of the new democracies encompass a diversity of national, religious, ethnic, and even racial groups. Ideas about citizenship that are based upon membership in such groups, rather than on the sovereignty of the individual, pose some of the gravest difficulties these countries face. Carl Gershman's contribution to the discussion that followed our world affairs panel on *America and the Democratic Revolution* was insightful and sobering. Our own society may be able to cope with the racial and ethnic balkanization that seems to be in fashion on some of our college campuses. But if these ideas take root in more fragile societies, the effects could be devastating.

- One of the deepest fears of the new democrats is the threat of social breakdown at the bottom: crime, family disintegration, corruption, communal violence, alcoholism, etc. When repressive government collapses, the basic fabric of society is suddenly exposed to terrible stresses. How the new democracies will manage this moral challenge is unclear, but neither the values of our yuppie "Me Generation" nor those of our permissive left-liberalism will be helpful. How the new democracies cope with their moral problems could, however, be instructive for us.

- It is possible that a new literary and artistic sensibility will emerge from the new democracies. It is hard to imagine that their experience will dispose them toward either the traditionalism of a dimly remembered past, or the destructive cynicism of what we call the post-modern period.

In sum, we are asking not only what the United States can do to make the most of the new democratic moment in the wider world. We are also asking if there is the possibility that this new moment could inspire civic and cultural renewal here at home, and what such a renewal might look like. Perhaps our country need not choose between expending its energies in world affairs and restoring its strength at home. Perhaps, as is often the case, by engaging with the world we will discover our own truer and stronger self.

Opening Dinner:
IS THIS A NEW MOMENT?

Chair: Rita Freedman
Stephen Solarz
William Phillips

Rita Freedman

The letter inviting you here didn't assert that this is a new moment. It rather asked us all if we thought it might be. We ourselves are not sure, and we look forward to hearing some opinions of the particularly qualified speakers.

Stephen Solarz

Congressman Stephen J. Solarz (D-NY), a member of the House Foreign Affairs and Intelligence Committees and Chairman of the Subcommittee on Asian and Pacific Affairs, has been a leading Congressional spokesman on behalf of democracy and human rights. Congressman Solarz was a floor leader during the House vote in support of "Operation Desert Storm."

Is this a new moment? Let us consider some omens.

In the *Village Voice*, a neighborhood weekly in New York, my support for the President's efforts to effectuate the liberation of Kuwait caused me to be characterized as a "loathsome, benighted incubus whose reptilian visage has darkened the airways with deadening regularity."

I can tell that most of you have about as much an idea what an incubus is as I did when I first read that column.   Under the assumption that I was being criticized, not complimented, I thought that I ought to find out what it means.   So I went to my dictionary and discovered that an incubus is an evil apparition which has sexual intercourse with sleeping women.   I must say that, even in Washington, I know of no one else who has been accused of such a thing.

But if the mood of some *Village Voice* writers remains unchanged, other aspects of our world are less bound to pattern. During the last two years, the world in which we live has been incredibly and irreparably changed. From Stettin in the Baltic to Trieste in the Adriatic, the Iron Curtain has ascended all across Europe. And lest anyone doubt the profundity of these changes, I have here a most dramatic manifestation of a world turned upside down.   It is the card of the former White House correspondent of *Trybuna Ludu,* which some of you may remember as the *Pravda* of Poland.   Next to the name *Trybuna Ludu,* he has penciled in the phrase, "Number one opposition paper of Poland."

The Warsaw Pact has collapsed.   The Cold War has ended.   Iraq annexed Kuwait, which was then liberated by a global coalition which was tolerated, if not supported, by the Soviet Union and the People's Republic of China. I thought it might be useful to talk about the implications of these developments and the changes they have wrought in the world for the future of U.S. foreign policy.   I would also like to advance seven points which might guide U.S. foreign policy in the future.

First, even after the Cold War, it is clear that we still live in an unsafe and unstable world where ethnic conflicts, religious rivalries, ambitions and acts of terrorism will create challenges to fundamental American values.

Secondly, a strong defense will remain a necessary condition for the protection or our most vital interests.

Third, the best way to preserve the peace is through the principle of collective security, rather than through the implementation of a *Pax Americana*. For a *Pax Americana*, we have neither the political will nor the necessary resources -- human and material. But for collective security we do, although we need to recognize

that American leadership will be as absolutely essential as it was in the Gulf.

Fourth, the use of direct force as a way of resolving the challenges we face should generally be a last resort. But use of force as a last resort is not the same as never. We need to recognize that there are times when the use of force is not only justified, it is necessary. This is a lesson embedded in the history of our own republic. Had it not been for the Revolutionary War, we would not have gained our independence. Had it not been for the Civil War, the Union would not have been preserved, and the slaves would not have been freed. Had it not been for World War II, the Third Reich might indeed have lasted for 1000 years. And had it not been for the war in the Gulf, a brutal despot would have had his hands on the economic jugular of the world. Because of his biological and nuclear weapons, Saddam Hussein would have been in a position to pursue his desires throughout the Middle East. The stage would surely have been set for additional campaigns of confrontation and conquest in the region.

Fifth, if force does have to be used, it is far better to use it openly, with the prior approval and authorization of Congress. In the case of the Gulf, our system worked exactly the way the framers of the Constitution designed it to work. The decision to go forward was not made by the President alone, but by the President and Congress together. As a result, it acquired a political legitimacy which it would not otherwise have had. One week after hostilities commenced, there were 75,000 anti-war demonstrators in Washington. Had the President gone to war without the approval of Congress, there no doubt would have been 750,000 demonstrators in the capital. At the same time that there were forces in the field trying to get Saddam out of Kuwait, a serious effort would have been underway to get George Bush out of the White House.

Sixth, if one aspect of the New World Order is an emerging consensus among the countries of the world that we must all recognize and enforce the sanctity of existing borders, another aspect must be the recognition that governments do not have an international entitlement to transform areas within their own borders into the equivalent of free fire zones, from which they can assault their own people. The principle of non-intervention in the internal affairs of other countries, while generally applicable, must not become a rationalization for paralysis.

When a government which lacks democratic legitimacy engages in a campaign of mass murder against its own people, the international community has a responsibility to do something about it. The international community would have been morally justified in taking action against Nazi Germany. It would also have been justified in talking action against Idi Amin in Uganda, Pol Pot in Cambodia and Saddam Hussein.

Finally, we need to recognize the truth in Victor Hugo's observation that, "There is no power so great as an idea whose time has come." In the last decade of the 20th century, after the failure of Fascism and the collapse of Communism, the aspiration of men and women to be free is the most powerful idea of our time. Therefore, the promotion of democratic political development should replace the containment of Communism as the foundation for a new American foreign policy.

Our job as participants in this dialogue is to transform these truths into concrete diplomatic, political and military action. This will require the energy, commitment, ideals and idealism of all of you here tonight, and all those who participate in this conference.

William Phillips

William Phillips has been the Editor of Partisan Review *for over fifty years, and is one of America's leading literary and political critics. He is a Professor of English at Boston University, and served as a member of President Carter's Task Force for the Arts and Humanities and on the Governor of New Jersey's Commission on the Arts. Mr. Phillips has written many books and articles, among them his autobiography --* A Partisan View: Five Decades of the Literary Life.

Fellow centrists: It is a pleasure to speak tonight to a gathering of people who share some political and cultural assumptions and are free of cant and knee-jerk responses. Whenever I discuss politics with more than several friends or with academic colleagues, there is usually a politically correct person who, after *not* listening to me, calls me a conservative, a warmonger, or a Reaganite. I have been assured that there are no politically correct people here tonight.

Of course, the opposite of politically correct is not politically incorrect. It is politically open. And that is how I would characterize the grouping of people at this meeting: we want to broaden the community situated between the dogmatists and extremists at either end of the political spectrum.

New ideas and cultural and political changes usually emerge at those moments when a group senses new opportunities, is fed up with the prevailing clichés, and develops a new perspective. I believe we are at such a moment.

I think all or most of us here would agree that the time is ripe. We are at the end of one historical period, and entering another. We are in what could be called a transitional phase. We might disagree on some aspects of the past and some of the directions in which we want to move. But I think some things are clear to us all.

We are seeing the end of Communism, if not the end of history. (The end of history had a short life.) The ideals of freedom, democracy and of the free market -- which so far seems to be a necessary condition for the others -- are once more held aloft in word if not always in practice.

The mood of the country has changed dramatically. We have emerged from the Vietnam doldrums. The swift and successful campaign in the Gulf has lifted the spirit of the country. True enough, after the brilliant victory, the Gulf situation seems to be slipping. There are bound to be some missteps. But the shift, overall, is undeniable.

There are signs that the cultural blight that has invaded the academy and the media is slowly receding. Though large and influential sections of both are still in the grip of politically correct ideas, today independent voices, free of entrenched interests and stock responses, are beginning to be heard. In the political arena, some politicians are questioning the old platitudes. This is the momentum that brings us here.

But we still are not out of the woods. The mainstream of our culture is largely a mélange of old diluted and distorted leftist attitudes. This is a significant phenomenon, because culture influences politics. Antonio Gramsci, the Italian Communist who spent most of his life polishing Marxist theory while in jail, made the point: whoever wins the culture of a country wins its politics.

One of our main problems is the split between the culture of the general population and the culture of the educated classes in the professions, the media, and the academy. This division has come about largely because the educated classes have absorbed some outworn, mildly leftish ideas, while the rest of the country, which has not been so affected, is motivated mostly by old-fashioned common sense, naive populism, and traditional moral and political values. This divide often results in a paralyzing polarization.

The educated, or, I should say, the more formally educated classes, have also been polarized into left and right, with the left much more numerous and stronger than the right. The center, to cite Yeats's famous line, has not held too well. And recently, the far right has resurfaced a new isolationism, with a measure of hostility to Israel, and traces of anti-Semitism. Patrick Buchanan's recent columns, in which he attacks the neoconservatives, are prime symptoms of this distressing phenomenon.

So a vague but inauthentic radical outlook still dominates the culture of the academy, the media, and the educated classes. To do something about this situation, one must have some idea why and how it came to pass. However, it is a complex matter, and there is no simple or single explanation.

I am using the term "culture" advisedly, because what has taken hold of the so-called educated classes are not simply wayward, or foolish, or backward opinions. What we have is actually a whole culture, in the anthropological sense of the word. Like French or German or English culture, it is rooted in common assumptions, aspirations, and pretensions, and inter-related theories. It is based also on certain notions of social goals, utopian visions, ways of life, and sexual values. It is something enveloping.

This is why arguing with someone whose head is embedded in this world of ideas and opinions rarely

gets you anywhere. You are not disputing distinct
opinions, you are actually arguing with hidden assumptions. In fact, specific opinions within this mind-
set sometimes vary and change. But they nevertheless
do not stray beyond its established boundaries.

What does this subculture consist of? And how has
it come into being? The prevailing set of beliefs is
often referred to as postmodernism: the conglomeration
of ideas, theories, values, assumptions, that displaced
an earlier phase commonly referred to as modernism.

Let me list a few
of its ingredients: a
belief in a widespread
relativism in moral,
political, and philoso-
phical matters; a com-
mitment to social
change, vaguely remi-
niscent of old radical
doctrines; a theoreti-
cal emphasis on

rights as against duties; a belief in unrestricted personal freedom, particularly in sexual matters; a general
rejection of the existing social system; a radical revision
of academic curricula; with an atmosphere of leftism
and anti-Americanism permeating the whole.

What are some of the specific theories and movements?

To begin with, there is deconstruction, a French
import, made famous by Jacques Derrida and by Paul
de Man. Today this is waning, but it has had a strong
influence on academic thinking.

At the risk of oversimplifying, the main tenets of
this school could be summed up as an emphasis on
relativism, on the conversion of thought and experience
into texts, and on the indeterminacy of meaning of all
texts. Deconstruction has allied itself with academic
Marxism, most notably in the works of Fredric Jameson
and Terry Eagleton, and a number of less famous
professors and epigones.

Then, of course, there is the strong feminist movement, which began as a champion of equal rights for women, and was supported by most sensible people. But feminism proliferated into a vast array of literary and social theories, based on all kinds of assumptions. Some of these took a very extreme view of the role of gender in art and society, and have been questioned by many writers and literary critics. They also involve a fierce assault on so-called white, male art and culture.

The field also includes black studies, which began with the movement for equal rights for blacks -- again, something supported by most sensible people. But one of the several streams that developed out of this was not only an elevation of black writing and African culture, but a put-down of so-called white European culture.

In addition, there is the powerful agitation for affirmative action, which began as an attempt to gain equal rights for women and blacks, but was transformed into preferential treatment for some of them. Then there is multiculturalism, which uses the fact that there are different cultural experiences to deny the centrality of the Western and American traditions -- and the need to teach them in our schools. Together, all these combine in an attack on the academic curriculum and on the traditions of Western civilization, dismissing it as the creation of dead white males.

This climate of opinion, it must be said, is not Marxist or socialist. But it has a radical accent. It is a kind of watered-down version of classic Marxism and socialist doctrine, divorced from the old revolutionary agenda. It clings to a spirit of radicalism that is anti-American and anti-capitalist, and vaguely pointed toward a different kind of society. That society is not clearly outlined or specified.

Why does this amalgam of ideas with a left veneer not only persist but command the passionate support of some members of the intelligentsia -- in the face of the demise of Utopian thinking? Why does it persist, when you consider that many of its assumptions and conclusions make no sense if they are examined systematically?

The only explanation of this historical phenomenon, it seems to me, is that since the French Revolution, bolstered by the influence of the Russian Revolution, the belief has persisted that it is more moral and more politically virtuous to be somewhere on the left -- and it doesn't really seem to matter where.

This helps explain the air of self-righteousness, dogmatism, and superiority that is characteristic of the people who uphold and propagate what I have been describing as the dominant culture of the academy, the media and the educated classes. Its appeal is further enhanced by the posture of being for the underprivileged -- an appeal that seems to facilitate the absorption of many questionable ideas.

In addition, I think that its standard-bearers in the academy make up a new self-perpetuating ideological bureaucracy. They have captured a number of departments and administrative posts, and not only influence educational policy, but also -- and this is of prime importance -- control new appointments.

I am emphasizing the importance of the new academic sub-culture because, as I have said, in a further diluted form it has spread to the media, the professions, and even to some of our political leaders in both parties (more, I must say, to the Democrats).

How can we oppose this ideological conglomeration? To begin with, we cannot take a purely negative attitude. Nor can we call simply for a return to traditional moral, political, and educational values.

Of course, we will be called conservatives or reactionaries by mindless people -- no matter what we say or do. They will insist that we are politically incorrect. But we should not give them any justification for the *ad hominem* use of political tags. Perhaps we can best counter such charges by continuing to do superior work in our own fields.

It is no exaggeration to say we are facing a genuine crisis in our culture. But at least one reason for optimism might be that ideological fashions do not last long in this country. Since the thirties, I have seen many changes in the cultural *zeitgeist*, and right now it is hard to believe that the current modes of trendy thinking are here to stay.

Keynote:
AMERICA AND THE NEW WORLD ORDER

Chair: Ronald Radosh
Charles Krauthammer

Ronald Radosh

Our first speaker, Charles Krauthammer, has received the Pulitzer Prize for Distinguished Commentary, and also the First Amendment Award from People for the American Way.

Charles is one of the surprisingly large group of Washington figures who still identify themselves as Scoop Jackson Democrats. I am beginning to do research on a book about the Democratic Party, and I was able to go to Washington State to read the recently-released Scoop Jackson papers. I learned a lot about what Scoop Jackson said and thought. He represented the integrity of traditional American liberalism. He believed in civil rights. He believed that when the U.S. was threatened, the U.S. had to stand up to defend its interests. These are views shared by many of us here today.

Charles Krauthammer

Charles Krauthammer is a Pulitzer Prize-winning columnist for The Washington Post Writers Group. He is a Contributing Editor of The New Republic, and served on the speech-writing staff of Vice President Walter Mondale.

I am glad to celebrate this new moment with you.

We are living through momentous events. The most recent was the Gulf War: an astonishing display of U.S. power. Another was the end of the Cold War: an astonishing display of Soviet collapse. And, third, we have seen the end of the most ideological century in human history, and the collapse of the last great collectivist utopianism. We have seen the death of socialism as an idea.

All three of these events conspired to create a new moment which presents to America two great challenges: one in foreign affairs and one in domestic affairs. One has to do with the role of America in the world, the other has to do with the nature of American society.

Let me start with the following challenge. It is clear that, after the collapse of the Soviet Empire, we are now looking at a unipolar world, with America at its apex. It was once predicted that a multipolar world system would replace the old bipolar system. Germany, Japan, and/or Europe would emerge as the new centers, sharing power with the U.S. and a diminished Soviet Union/Russia. No doubt a multipolarity such as this will come in time -- perhaps after another generation there will be great powers co-equal with the U.S. But we are not there now, nor will we be for decades. Now is the unipolar moment.

The myth of a multilateral system was resoundingly exploded during the Gulf War. It was the end of the Cold War that changed the structure of the world, but it was the Gulf War that revealed that change. What the Gulf War revealed was that there is only one superpower now, the United States. There may be a number of secondary powers, most prominent among them the Soviet Union. Germany and Japan, although clearly economic superpowers, are only secondary players on the international scene.

In 20 or 30 years we will undoubtedly be living in a multipolar world. We cannot maintain a unipolar system forever. But today, the U.S. is the only country with the military, diplomatic, economic and political assets to exercise a decisive influence in any part of the world. So we have to abandon the myth of multipolarity.

The second myth has to do with American decline. Before the Gulf War, American declininsts were lamenting America's fall from world leadership. The benchmark year they always measured from was 1950. So let's look at 1950. In 1950, the U.S. was engaged in a war with North Korea. It lasted two years, cost 54,000 American lives, and ended in a draw. Forty-one years later the U.S. entered a war with Iraq, a country comparable in size: it lasted six weeks, cost 196 American lives, and ended in a rout. If the Roman Empire had declined at this rate, I would be addressing you in Latin.

"Ah ha!" you say "There is a big difference between the war in Iraq and the war in Korea." That is precisely the point. In 1950, our adversaries had strategic depth, with the whole Communist world behind them. That is why we had great difficulty winning in Korea and Vietnam. Forty years later, with our one great adversary in disarray, our enemies in the world no longer have such depth. When we do encounter enemies like Saddam, they have to face us on their own. They don't stand a chance. That is just the difference between Iraq and Korea. Victory in the Cold War, the neutralization of our giant geopolitical adversary, has resulted in our preeminence. We are in the unipolar world.

It is clear, of course, that if America succeeds in running its economy into the ground, it will forfeit its unipolar dominance. There is a theory that attributes our decline to too great an involvement overseas, and too much spending on defense. It seems to be irrepressible. I will give you just one number. We are now spending 5.4 percent of our GNP on defense. Under John Kennedy, we were spending almost twice as much, and that was when the U.S. was at its economic and political apogee. Under the current projections for defense spending by the Republican administration, we will be spending less than 4 percent on defense in the next decade -- our lowest level since Pearl Harbor.

Recognizing the unipolar structure of the world is one thing, but accepting it is another. Americans have a very long history of being uncomfortable with projecting our power and influence abroad. I'm talking about the isolationist impulse, which I think is strong, and I predict will be strong in the future. The isolationist movement reached its apogee in the 1930s, and remained, if somewhat restrained, even during the forty years of the Cold War. At the end of the Cold War, when it was clear that the Soviet Union and Eastern Europe would collapse, there was a rush among isolationists in the U.S. Congress to declare a peace dividend, which was another way of promoting disarmament. At a White House press conference in February, 1990, Colin Powell was asked whether a $300 billion defense budget was really necessary. Helen Thomas asked, "Who is the enemy?" Well, three months later we got the answer. Saddam has reminded us that the world is a nasty place, even without the Soviet threat. Americans don't appreciate this reminder. We promptly look for evasions to escape our responsibilities as a super-power.

There are essentially two kinds of evasions. The first is multilateralism. One way to escape the crushing burdens of being a superpower is to say, let the U.N. Security Council and the notion of "collective security" take care of the world. We're due to retire.

Many who put their faith in multilateralism draw strength from the Gulf War experience. I believe, however, that they profoundly misinterpret what happened in the Gulf War. It was not an act of collective security; it was an example of Anglo-American unilateralism. Without the U.S. cajoling, and the U.S. and the British carrying the bulk of the fighting, there would have been no resistance, no embargo, and there would now be no Kuwait. Saddam would control a crucial region of the world.

Multilateralism is a nice idea, but an impractical one. Collective security cannot guarantee our security or that of friends in the world. It can be a dangerous illusion, because it allows us to abdicate our own responsibilities to what is essentially a paper organization.

After all, multilateralism does not even make sense in terms of the American national interest. Taking multilateralism seriously means inviting China, France and the U.S.S.R. -- countries, indifferent, if not hostile, to our interests -- to have a decisive say, indeed a veto, over our interests and those of our friends. Why a great power, particularly a hegemonic power, would do that is a puzzle to me.

If we want relative stability and tranquility in the world, we are going to have to work for it. It will neither come by itself, nor as a gift from the Security Council. It will only come if the United States shapes the New World Order.

If the first danger is multilateralism, the second is isolationism. We saw very interesting examples of this problem during the Gulf War. In fact, we began to see a rather new kind of isolationism. We are familiar with the isolationism of the left, the reaction to the Vietnam War. But for almost 50 years we had not seen the isolationism of the right. It is clear to me that for many on the right, Communism was a particular ideological and practical threat, and, now that it seems to have been dealt with, we can return to the old isolationism. Many of the old right have been quite candid about this. It began with a Tory speech by Russell Kirk at the Heritage Foundation a few years ago, in which he leveled a rather vicious attack against "globalism." It has been followed up in the popular press by Patrick Buchanan, who, when the Cold War ended a year and a half ago, wrote that it is time for America to "come home."

It is interesting to note that the push for isolationism today is not coming from the left. After all, those who were propelled toward isolationism after the Vietnam War are already there. What is new, and where I believe we will see the great growth area of isolationism, is on the right, where isolationism was almost entirely suppressed during the Cold War era. As a result of the Gulf War, right-wing isolationism has in some ways been discredited. But as the memory of the Gulf War fades, and as America's unipolar status becomes more evident, I expect there will be growing intellectual support for this isolationism of the right.

One way to look at our situation is to say, left isolationism fears to engage the world because it fears that America will corrupt the world, while right isolationism refuses to engage the world because it fears that the world will corrupt America. These two strains of isolationism will probably produce alliances in the future that will confound all ideological distinctions.

I don't want to overstate the moral case against isolationism. But when we tried it as a practical matter in the 1930s, we had a catastrophe. If the world were still as it was a hundred years ago, isolationism might have some real appeal. But the relative tranquility enjoyed in the 19th century was not an historical accident, it was a result of the British Navy patrolling the two great oceans. Alas, the British Navy is gone, and our navy is standing in its place. So we need to recognize that international stability is never a given; it is never the norm. It comes through the self-conscious action of great powers. If America wants stability, it will have to create it.

We should recognize that there is a new and very ominous threat to international stability. We are entering an era of mass destruction, a revolutionary age of technology. The fact that many small countries are acquiring weapons of mass destruction is the greatest threat we face in the coming decade. The Pentagon estimates that by the year 2,000 two dozen countries will have ballistic missiles, seven or eight will have nuclear weapons, thirty will have chemical weapons, ten will have biological weapons.

It has become a cliche to say that modern technology has shrunk the world. The corollary may not be so apparent: this technological shrinkage will blur the distinction between regional superpowers and great powers. Missiles shrink distance. Nuclear and chemical weapons multiply power. Both can now be bought at the market. Fifty years ago, Germany disturbed the peace of the world. Germany was centrally located, highly industrial and heavily populated. Fifty years later, it took only an Iraq to disturb the peace of the world.

Iraq is the prototype of this new strategic threat. North Korea is next on the list. Tomorrow it could be Libya, Pakistan, Iran, South Africa -- it is hard to say which. And one of the reasons why we need to stay engaged in the world is that we are the only power that can deal with threats like this.

Another problem is the rise of aggressive nationalisms like the kind we are seeing in the Soviet empire. These pose a slightly different threat, because the way these countries will develop is an open question right now. But their emergence forces us to face new questions, and to make new rules.

For example, what can we do about the Georgians? The Armenians? We face some similar problems in responding to the Kurds and the Palestinians. We need new ideas to deal with the questions of the powerlessness of whole peoples, and the problems of reconstituting sovereign states.

I would like to deal with one other challenge which is facing us at this new moment: a challenge we face at home. The collapse of socialism as a moving force in the world may have some far-reaching implications. If the threat to America's position in the world will come from right-wing isolationists, the threat to America's position at home will probably come from the left. The reason is that the collapse of socialism has created great bewilderment on the left. After all, socialism was a kind of religion of the left. The decay of this religion has brought the problem of how to sustain the passions of the left. One possibility for those who oppose what we call democratic capitalism is that they will drop the proletariat and take up the causes of racial, ethnic, and other kinds of minorities. This raises the problem of what can be called the balkanization of America. It involves the possible breakdown of two very cherished notions, American culture and American citizenship.

America alone among the multiethnic countries of the world has managed to assimilate its citizenry into a common nationality.   I believe that we are now doing our best to squander this great achievement. We accomplished it by being carefully federalist in our politics, and by having a powerful melting-pot culture.   Most important, we have dealt with the problem of ethnic diversity by embracing a radical individualism, and by rejecting notions of group rights.   There has been one great, shameful historical exception: the denial of rights to American blacks. When that exception was outlawed in the 1960s, America appeared to be ready to resume its destiny, a destiny celebrated by Martin Luther King as the home of a true and universal individualism.

Why is this destiny celebrated?   Because it works.   Every other country that has tried to deal with ethnic issues by creating group rights has suffered as a result.   You can see this everywhere: from India to Beirut to Iraq, and even in a peaceful country like Canada.   The irony is that most of these multiethnic societies now coming to grief because of their separatisms look to the U.S. as a model of how to develop a common citizenship and identity.   But we are now in the process of throwing away our great achievement.

The attack on the American model takes two forms.   First, it challenges the idea of a common Western culture, and, secondly, it challenges the idea of a common American citizenship.   It begins with a new definition of oppression.   The oppressed are no longer the working classes, they are a new class of carefully selected ethnic and gender groups: Blacks, Hispanics, women, homosexuals, Native Americans -- the list is long, and the bids are open.

In their name is launched an all-out assault, first on America's cultural past.   The demand is not for a justifiable expansion of the West's cultural canon to include appropriate works by women or people of color. It is rather for the destruction of this canon as representative of a white, male-dominated system of cultural oppression. This is not only happening at universities, but it is being pushed into the grade schools. Many of you are familiar with a proposed revision of New York State's school curriculum to rid it of "Eurocentric" bias. This is clearly a demand by vigorous pressure groups for what is called "ethnic cheerleading." It was protested by historians who included Diane Ravitch, Arthur Schlesinger, Jr., C. Van Woodward, Robert Caro and some 20 others not known for their ideological similarities.

The other attack is on the idea of a common citizenship. This involves the division of Americans into a hierarchy of legally preferred groups based on race and gender. Every other country, from Canada to Lebanon, that has attempted such racial and tribal stratification has regretted it. At least some of those countries have a kind of social structure that allows the possible option of partition. If separatism doesn't work in Canada, for example, Quebec could secede. But in our country, partition is not an option.

It seems in this new moment we have some remarkable challenges. I am particularly concerned about our domestic challenge. It poses a threat no outside power could possibly impose. As a great power we can make mistakes abroad, and still survive -- as we did in Vietnam -- to be left with just the scars. We won't disappear. But if we take the wrong road at home, if we misunderstand the nature of the American idea and fracture our tradition of citizenship, we may not come out as well.

Discussion

ROBERT KUTTNER: That, of course, was brilliant. I agree with about ninety percent of it. But I wonder if I could press on two matters? First, on the domestic front: as you tick off the elements of the assault on citizenship and on Americanness -- both of which I quite agree about -- why do you leave out the attack on the polity from the right? Isn't there also a threat from the quarter which argues that the state can do nothing right, the polity can do nothing right, and the market can do nothing wrong? Second, where do you come down on the relationship between geopolitical assertiveness and economic assertiveness? If Germany and Japan are exporting bad things to predatory Third World countries, if they do not accept the same international trade rules that we follow, what do we do about it? Get into a trade war? What is the right balance between geo-economic assertiveness and geopolitical self-restraint?

CHARLES KRAUTHAMMER: On the first issue I think you're absolutely right. There is a parallel assault on our common citizenship which comes from the right. It has this skepticism about the state, and a complete faith in the free market. But I don't emphasize this problem because the right is entirely hypocritical. Those who sincerely hold this view are a very small minority, and are nowhere in power: the libertarians, for instance -- a somewhat cranky group. Whenever our conservatives achieve state power, they wield it rather happily, and whatever changes they make come pretty much at the margins. It would even be hard to characterize the results of the Reagan revolution as a radical disarming of the power of the state vis-a-vis the market or American society. It was perhaps a retrenchment of sorts, but the amount of economic protectionism conservatives bring about is comparable to what liberals are able to achieve; it's just done for a different set of interest groups. The assault from the left on the notion on common citizenship is much more genuine, and deserves to be taken more seriously. It has become unrelenting, and we can see it at all levels of our culture.

Another reason for emphasizing the threat from the left is that the conservative attack on the state and state intervention is a rather old idea: we've been having this argument for at least fifty years. But the challenge of ethnic, racial and gender separateness, although always out there in the culture, has suddenly gained much more power. We haven't yet developed the antibodies to deal with this, although we have done so for the anti-statism of the right.

On the issue of our geo-economic interests: that almost belongs in another discussion. It is difficult to deal with all of it. Clearly, we are not in a unipolar world in terms of economics. No one could possibly claim that we have the control over the world economic system that we had in 1950. But how you deal with Saddam and nuclear weapons is a very different matter from how you deal with GATT. Dealing with the economic problems we have with other democratic countries obviously can't be done in a high-handed way.

CORD MEYER: How should the United States assert its power when it comes to the proliferation of nuclear weapons? Don't we have to rely on some form of improved international structure, and policing authority? Or do we try to do it all by ourselves?

CHARLES KRAUTHAMMER: If we can create international structures to do the job, then let's do it. In most cases I think it's a pipe dream to believe that multilateral agencies can do this. Iraq has now been disarmed twice of its nuclear weapons, and it was not done by the International Atomic Energy Commission. It was done by the Israeli Air Force and the American Air Force. Clearly, of course, one of the models to follow is the approach we took to Saddam: try to create an international coalition; try to develop whatever other mechanisms you can, short of the use of force; try to use every conceivable kind of pressure. But I have absolutely no doubt that, had we not in the end been willing to act alone, Iraq would soon have been in control of the entire Arabian peninsula.

In the end, we have to be prepared to act -- if necessary, militarily and unilaterally. I am not, of course, suggesting we can do this when there are violations of the GATT agreements, or when petty conflicts break out somewhere such as Yugoslavia. But where vital interests and values are concerned, we have to be ready to do the job ourselves. And we have been. I think that it is pretty clear that we have been acting illegally in taking over a part of Iraq to help spare the Kurds. Because it had to be done. I am sure we can now round up the usual international lawyers to find the legal justifications for what we did. But in the moment of crisis, we simply had to act -- or the Kurds would have been driven out for good.

BERNARD ARONSON: Charles, I agree with you about the threat of balkanization to our country. There are two things that are interesting about this phenomenon. One thing is how rapidly it has developed, and how powerful it is. The second thing is how unpopular it is: not just in the culture, but in our political life. This is a bad political idea, not a winning political idea. Both political parties are afraid of it, and yet it has power.

We have to work on developing antibodies to ward off and destroy this threat. This will take some thought. First, in any political contest the side that captures the moral language has an enormous advantage. In this battle the left has for the moment captured the moral language. I think that we need to begin to think very hard about a language of citizenship and nationhood that can redefine this debate.

CHARLES KRAUTHAMMER: You can't fight something with nothing. It is not very hard to come out against balkanization. But when the left is arguing for separatism as a way to cure racial injustice, the argument gets a lot harder. The left has insulated itself from attack by wrapping itself in the appeal to racial justice. Our response, I think, has to be that we are as committted to achieving racial and ethnic justice and harmony as they are. But we reject this particular approach as catastrophic to the American ideal.

First, we need to show how separatism can destroy our country. I grew up in Canada, and if you ask Canadians about cultural separation, they will tell you how much grief it has brought them. And Canada's situation is much simpler than ours! Quebec is, after all, geographically separate. Here, where geographic separatism isn't a solution, it can only end in civil disintegration.

Second, one has to offer some positive ideas about how to overcome real injustices. Let me posit a very simple proposition, although I have not thought it through. Why not have a kind of affirmative action based wholly on need, without any reference to ethnicity, gender, or race? Children could be helped simply on the basis their economic status, or a demonstrated need for remedial education, health care, or whatever. This would, no doubt, run into difficulties. But they are likely to be less grave than those we are discovering when we hand out goodies on the basis of skin color or gender. There are surely ways to reclaim some of the moral high ground from the left -- whose claims, after all, are very shaky.

STEVEN MORRIS: You stated at the beginning the argument that Communism is dead -- Communism being the last great messianic ideology of this century of ideologies. You then went on to suggest that the main challenge likely to come in the future will be from regimes that have weapons of mass destruction. You ran off a checklist of possible threats: North Korea, Libya, Iran, etc.

But isn't it the case that the characteristic of all these regimes is that they are despotisms shaped by messianic ideologies: Communism in North Korea; pan-Arabism and Islam in the case of Libya and Iraq; fundamentalism in Iran, and so on? In fact, isn't the problem we face from these regimes not that they possess destructive weapons, but the kinds of people who run these countries, and the extremist ideologies the rulers promote?

CHARLES KRAUTHAMMER: It's an interesting idea, but I have some problems with it. Saddam concocted all kinds of ideologies. He tried pan-Arabism, he tried Islamic fundamentalism, at times he tried a kind of poor man's Marxism. I have no doubt that such leaders will try to create messianic ideologies to justify their depredations, but I wouldn't take them seriously. I'm not sure many other people do, either. Libya has one of the weirdest ideologies around. It's almost incomprehensible to Libyans -- a green revolution in a country where few people even know what green is. All they've seen is sand.

What we're looking at, generally speaking, is what used to be the called crazy states. What these countries have in common is not so much a messianic ideology, but a kind of one man, one party regime *a la* Hitler. Because of this centralization of power, the regime is able to do horrible things, which wouldn't be tolerated in most other countries.

North Korea, Iraq and Libya are in that category. But other dangerous states I mentioned are Iran, Pakistan, and South Africa. These are countries with far more liberal political systems, if you will; there is far more popular constraint. It's hard to imagine any of those three states becoming a Saddam-like state overnight. One real problem is that we are in a new technological era, comparable to the advent of air power. And we are so early in the process -- it is like 1911. Just how the process will unfold is hard to see, but I suspect our children are going to see it all too clearly.

RONALD RADOSH: Charles, thank you so much for your wonderful presentation.

AMERICA AND THE DEMOCRATIC REVOLUTION

Chair: Robert Leiken
Joshua Muravchik, Paul Berman
James LeMoyne, Bernard Aronson

Robert Leiken

Like the rest of our colleagues, I am a veteran of the fierce debate waged over Central America in chambers like this one during the 1980s. Indeed, if this panel had been convened as recently as two years ago, it doubtless would have been in the expectation of yet another battle over Central American policy. Probably our voices and many of those in the audience would have been raised in anger.

But no matter how loud our voices might have been, few Americans would have been listening to us. Because in May of 1989, they would have been glued to their TV sets in wonder as hundreds of thousands of Chinese students, workers and other ordinary Chinese citizens paid homage to the goddess of democracy, an emblem of the universalized role of American democracy. During that first great day in what was to become a wonder year of democracy we were hardly aware that the exhausting war in Central America was coming to an end. Thanks to a bipartisan consensus that Bernie Aronson helped to forge, the American Congress was at last able to unite around the idea of democracy for Central America. Central American democrats had for decades been saying that only a bipartisan consensus in the U.S. could end the war of extremes in Central America.

It is not too great an exaggeration to say that the first peace in what Charles Krauthammer and Josh Muravchik are calling the *Pax Americana* was the unity of Americans around democracy. The goddess of democracy in Tiananmen, and the election celebrations in Central Europe which Paul Berman has written about so eloquently, are also an embodiment of what unites us as Americans. But what the new democrats elsewhere revere in us we often barely notice ourselves, being so preoccupied by our internal conflicts and debates.

Perhaps that is one reason for the lack of depth in the American response to the democratic revolution, which Penn Kemble called to our attention last night. But it is a measure of how much has changed in the past two years that all of us are here today not to debate a war, but to have a conversation about the role of American democracy in a world made new by democracy.

Joshua Muravchik

Joshua Muravchik, a Resident Scholar at the American Enterprise Institute for Public Policy Research, has just published his third book, Exporting Democracy *(AEI Press). His previous works include* The Uncertain Crusade: Jimmy Carter and the Dilemmas of Human Rights Policy *and* News Coverage of the Sandinista Revolution.

Promoting democracy should be the centerpiece of U.S. foreign policy. Of course, the first goal of foreign policy is to secure our safety, and thus it is always essential to maintain our adequate military capability and the courage to use that when we need to. That's bedrock. But the higher goal ought to be to shape a global order in which we have to use our military might rarely, if at all. The best of strategies toward this goal is to promote democracy.

This is true for two main reasons. One is that the more democracies there are in the world, the more pro-American the world will be. Democratic governments are friendlier to America than dictatorships. Democratic governments are sometimes nuisances -- France, Sweden, India, and Costa Rica. But

no democratic government has ever been an enemy of ours. Secondly, democratic governments are more peaceful. They have often taken to arms, but almost always when the peace has first been broken by a dictatorship. We have no clear example in which two democratic governments have gone to war against one another.

I think this point has been underscored by those who have tried to challenge it. I have in mind Patrick Buchanan and other leaders of the American branch of *Pamyat*, who gave the example that in World War II democratic England declared war on non-democratic Finland. This is quite true. Finland, you recall, was allied with Nazi Germany, and Stalin began to put a great deal of pressure on Churchill to declare war. Finally, Churchill acquiesced, and declared war on Finland. But not a shot was fired. It is clearly an exception that proves the rule.

Too often we grant that work in the realm of ideas is a kind of a secondary or unimportant feature of our foreign policy. But the events of the last few years ought to have cured us of that illusion. We have just secured our most impressive victory ever as a nation: our victory in the Cold War against an opponent more formidable and threatening than any other we ever faced. We defeated this opponent in an almost bloodless victory that was won almost entirely in the realm of ideas. Bear in mind that the Soviet Union today has more nuclear warheads, more throwweight, more tanks, artillery, infantry and so on than we have. But they are dead in the water, because their idea is dead. There could be no more dramatic proof of the impact of ideas on concrete matters of national security.

The question has been raised whether it is *realistic* for us to further the spread of democracy. Those who know me will attest that there are a few people more skeptical than I am. But here I have to be skeptical of skepticism.

The skeptics say that most Third World countries have no democratic tradition. This seems to miss the very obvious point that no country has a democratic tradition before it has attained some level of democracy. That's how you get democratic tradition. It's true that in a small number of cases -- England, and countries that were settled by people from England -- you can say that the development of democracy was an extension of centuries of constitutional practice. But in the majority of countries that we think of today as well-established democracies, there was no democracy a few generations ago, and therefore not much democratic tradition. We should also remember that the same skepticism about democracy expressed today about various Third World countries was expressed not long ago about Japan, Germany, Italy and elsewhere, where democracy has taken root.

In 1776, the United States became the first democracy in the world. At that time our population was barely a few million. Slaves, women and people without property could not vote. The total electorate that launched this experiment in self-representation was less than a million. Today, some 2 billion people in more than 60 countries, some 40 percent of the world's population, live under democratic governments. That represents a radical transformation over a relatively short period of time in the way the world governs itself.

Is it possible for America to be the agency for the further expansion of democracy? The answer seems to me to be an obvious "yes." In fact, America has been the agency of much of the expansion of democracy that has occurred over these two hundred years. Sometimes this has simply been by the force of our example, which inspired the French Revolution, the British working men's clubs, and a variety of other democratic forces in Europe and Latin America. Sometimes it has proceeded by the force of arms -- in Germany, Japan, the Dominican Republic and Grenada. Sometimes we have assisted democracy through strenuous diplomatic intervention -- in the Philippines, Haiti, El Salvador, and South Korea. Sometimes we have assisted through the kinds of programs supported by the National Endowment for Democracy: our assistance to *Solidarnosc*, or the broadcasts that kept truth and hope alive in Eastern Europe.

What should we do now to further the process? A long list could be enumerated, but the main points can be reduced to these:

* Radically increase the budget for the National Endowment for Democracy;

* Launch a Radio Free Asia to do for China, North Korea and Vietnam what Radio Free Europe and Radio Liberty have done for the Soviet Union and Eastern Europe;

* Focus our diplomatic endeavors more clearly on promoting democracy, especially where our influence is strongly felt, as it is right now in the Persian Gulf;

• Press for democracy in the two most important non-democratic countries, the Soviet Union and China, both of which we've just discovered to be rich in indigenous democratic forces far beyond what any of us imagined to be the case a few years ago.

We must also struggle to free ourselves of spurious notions of realism and *realpolitik* in foreign policy -- the geopolitics which imagines the world as a kind of chessboard. We have to think only of the recent experience in the Persian Gulf to see what trouble and foolishness this thinking can lead us to. We kowtowed for a very long time to the government of Iraq because we saw it on the global chessboard as a counterweight to the government of Iran. We also humiliated ourselves by selling weapons to the government of Iran because we saw it on the grand chessboard as a counterweight to the government of Iraq. The overwhelming lesson of the 20th century is that our history is not shaped mechanistically, by pieces on the chessboard, but rather in the hearts and minds of people. The entire history of this century has been shaped by movements -- Communism, nationalism, Fascism -- which rallied the imagination. In so doing, these movements simply changed the chessboard -- changed queens into pawns, changed pawns into queens, or knocked the board over altogether, and rewrote the rules.

The classic statement of the realist position of foreign policy comes, ironically, from Stalin. He sneeringly asked, "How many divisions has the Pope?" In 1989 we got the answer to this question. Stalin's empire was brought to rubble by series a of events precipitated to a very great degree by the Pope.

Today Fascism and Communism have gone by the board, and it is becoming clear that the most powerful and enduring revolution of our century is the democratic revolution. We can say with pride that democracy is, to a large degree, America's gift to the world. It can also become our gift to ourselves, if we have the foresight to organize our foreign policy around it.

Paul Berman

Paul Berman, a fellow at the New York Institute for the Humanities at New York University, is a writer on politics and culture for The Village Voice *and other journals.*

I have four historical observations, drawn from a magazine the Democratic Party published in the days when the Democratic Party was a formidable intellectual enterprise. That was back in the 1840s. The magazine was *The Democratic Review*, and it was really first-rate. When you look at the writers associated with this magazine, the first thing you will notice is that the notion of a New World Order, or at least the notion that the United States has a message to bring to the world, was already well established. The origins of this idea go back far beyond Woodrow Wilson.

One of the writers for this magazine was Nathaniel Hawthorne: a Democratic Party figure, he traced the genealogy of the American democratic idea to the Protestant Reformation -- especially to the English Civil War. Another was Walt Whitman, who projected the idea forward. In fact, he predicted that in the period immediately following the American bicentennial, in our period right now, American democracy would dominate the world. Perhaps a better way to put it is that our ideas would interweave themselves into the thinking of the rest of the world.

Living in our times makes us aware that this idea of an American world destiny, however expressed, is truer in a more literal fashion than anyone, as far as I can see, ever imagined. It was an editor of *The*

Democratic Review, John Louis O'Sullivan,   who coined the phrase "Manifest Destiny." But the writers of *The Democratic Review* recognized that this idea embraced two rather different emphases.   One was an emphasis on expansion -- through force, if need be. I think the phrase *Pax Americana* fits into this interpretation of America's destiny.   It has a certain imperial ring.   It is this, in my view, that makes the idea of a *Pax Americana* a dangerous thing. Under an imperial *Pax*, the empire rules.

But there is another emphasis, which might be called *Pax Democratica*. This perspective allows for and encourages self-rule, because democracy must entail self-government. I was glad to see Congressman Solarz cringe at the phrase *Pax Americana*, and speak of the virtues of collective security. But something about the phrase *Pax Americana* was so intoxicating that, in the formulation of collective security offered by Congressman Solarz, we already hear about the legitimacy of going to war against Pol Pot and Idi Amin as well as Saddam Hussein. It occurred to me that, had we done all those worthy things, we would have been at war continuously over the past 30 years, and on three continents. So this idea seems to need further refining.

Whitman's alternative was for America to seek global success through economic and political achievements that would overcome competing systems. But when Whitman and other writers of the times spoke about this mission, they saw a deeper purpose. To them, peace and prosperity were the preconditions for an individualism of ordinary working people -- not an individualism that stands in contrast to ideas of solidarity, but an individualism of the working masses. Now it has been said at this meeting that democracy has lost its utopian appeal, and that today -- as Penn Kemble put it -- Americans seem to find it difficult to raise more than one cheer for democracy. While this may be true, it is worth remembering that the notion of individualism, as Whitman understood it, includes a spiritual quality. Whitman's notion of individualism was almost ideological. The pro-democratic writers of that time understood democracy in terms that were rooted in the English Civil War and the Reformation. Whitman believed that by achieving political and economic individuality, people could at last achieve full adulthood. By that they could approach what he called the universal.

This vein of thought has disappeared almost entirely from our own political language, yet you can find a perfect expression of it -- with uncanny parallels to Whitman -- in the letters and essays of Vaclav Havel.

Not all the democratic movements of the world have taken up this notion of spiritual individualism. Some countries turn to democracy on purely practical grounds, as Whitman always said they would. But I think that we should remind ourselves that democracy as a practical arrangement tends to be unstable. Countries may try it out; their attempts are only partial; prosperity does not follow; and the military or some other anti-democratic group takes over. To be stable, democracy must retain the ideal of religious-type transformation, a cult of individual freedom.

I don't believe that this is captured in the present discussion about a New World Order. Democracy must include elements of disorder if it is to be a truly transforming, radical idea. I think that in the present period the principal evidence of the spread of the democratic idea (as I think it needs to be understood) can be found in the worldwide popularity of American culture.

We don't even speak about this in our normal political discourse. But our movies, our music and our literature are full of this idea of radical individualism, and the spiritual aspect of the individual. The American counterculture of the Fifties and Sixties has, ironically, been remarkably successful in spreading these ideas. The popularity of the contemporary American counterculture in Central Europe is attributable, I think, to the fact it does contain these Whitmanesque ideas.

Now, how a foreign policy could usefully take these things into consideration is very hard to say. But it occurs to me that the spread of democracy is not, in the last analysis, a product of foreign policy. It is, rather, a product of this culture. The students of Tiananmen Square, or Havel's circle in Czechoslovakia, may not be figures to whom the practitioners of power politics are naturally attracted. But I think they are the basis of a future world *Pax Democratica*.

James LeMoyne

James LeMoyne, a widely-published journalist, is currently writing a book about the United States and Central America. From 1981 through 1989, he reported on Central America, first for Newsweek *and then for* The New York Times. *Most recently, he covered the Persian Gulf crisis for* The New York Times.

I've been thinking about the theme of the conference itself: Are we at a new moment in Central America? I've just come back from covering the Persian Gulf War from Saudi Arabia for *The New York Times*, and I'm really struck by the differences in the two experiences. In Central America, Western cultures, mutants of the Western family, are in one stage of a very long struggle to democratize. In

Saudi Arabia and Kuwait, I was struck by the fact
that a similar kind of self-perception and debate is
not under way. Between the two poles represented
by a society such as El Salvador and a society such
as Kuwait, there are many variations. The distinctions that must be drawn present the U.S. and others
who consider themselves democrats with a range of
options in foreign affairs. How deeply should we be
involved? What kind of conditions should we try to
impose through our assistance and trade policies?

I do share the sense that we are in a new
moment as a result of the end of the Cold War, and
that we have new possibilities. In Central America,
it has opened the possibilities of politics. The Latin
American policies of the United States have been in
deep contradiction in the years of the Cold War because we have often acted against our better self.
We felt we had to support secret police and armies in
order to defeat Communism. But the best people
involved in these policies knew at the same time --
Guatemala in 1954 provides the best example -- that
supporting such institutions would make it more
difficult for civil society to democratize itself.

Central America is at the point where democratization is very much on the agenda. The Cold War is
over: the issue is not militarizing civilians, but civil-
ianizing militaries. But in a place like Saudi Arabia
you soon discover that, with very few exceptions, they
don't have the first thought about the kinds of participation in society that make democracy possible.
In fact, they consider democracy to be deeply threatening, threatening to their identity. I don't think it's
appropriate for the United States to intervene too
vigorously in a society like that.

A few Saudi democrats said to me, "How is it that
you were so supportive of democrats in Nicaragua,
when your ambassador here won't even talk to us?"
So there are some real costs to a policy of non-intervention. In the 1970s Nicaraguans used to say to
me, "Why won't the U.S. Ambassador talk to us?

We're democrats." I didn't have any good answer for them.

My experience in Central America did leave me with some ideas about how the U.S. can use its influence in societies that do want to democratize. What it really comes down to is that elections do work. But it's a long process. America should have more patience than we normally demonstrate.

Nor should we be put off by the costs: it doesn't take great resources to encourage people who are democratically inclined to follow their own interests.

It's a mistake not to support the government of Nicaragua -- despite all its shortcomings and the enduring power of the Sandinistas -- as it gropes toward democracy. By the same token, it's a mistake to support the military in Guatemala when it resists democratization. It is now time for the U.S. to tell Latin American militaries that they're not our allies: they may have been necessary for a particular time, but now their future lies in democratizing. I don't think it's that difficult.

After all, many of them can see that capitalism works, and democracy works. We are at a point where we are winning the argument. It would be very foolish to win the argument in countries like El Salvador and Nicaragua, and then to walk away without making the modest commitments that need to be made to assure the survival of democratic institutions.

Let me conclude with a reminiscence of a moment that I found quite striking. During the contra peace talks in Central America, Oscar Arias once took me aside. He said, "You know, I've been in the deepest argument with the Reagan administration about what

is going on here. What I believe is that, if there is a
free election in Nicaragua, the Nicaraguan people will
vote against the Sandinistas. Nobody in the Reagan
administration seems to believe that. What I don't
understand is that I got this sense of what is happening from living in Boston and watching the Kennedy-
Nixon election. I really believe that, given the choice,
people will vote their common sense. Why doesn't
the Reagan administration see it this way?"

I thought about his question. What happened was
the Cold War. The Reagan administration became
convinced that the Sandinistas would never give the
Nicaraguan people a free choice. But Oscar Arias
turned out to have been right. And what happened
demonstrated that, when we can, we should simply
help to provide people with the chance to follow their
common sense. We should have faith in them --
because they'll generally do the sensible thing.

Bernard Aronson

*Bernard Aronson is the Assistant Secretary of State
for Latin American and Caribbean Affairs. His articles have appeared in many magazines and op-ed
pages.*

I'd like to offer several observations on the topic
we were asked to address: America, democracy and
the New World Order.

First, what we have been witnessing over the past
several years is something that goes far beyond politics. It is commonly referred to as a "democratic revolution." That is an accurate, but not an adequate,
description. I think what we've seen is a reaffirma-
tion of the human spirit against some of the greatest
forces ever arrayed in history to crush it. If we had
gathered here five years ago to talk about the future

of totalitarianism and Communism, none of us would even have begun to imagine what we've witnessed in the last two years.

We believed that Communism in the Soviet Union was built on an authoritarian tradition in Russian culture and would endure for generations. We might have conceded that in Poland there was some hope, because nationalism could be harnessed against Communism through the Catholic Church and Solidarity. But we would have said that East Germany had become a rigid police state that probably would not be undone for a hundred years. Yet we have all seen that in the course of the last two years the whole system has collapsed like a house of cards. The lesson to me is that there is something indomitable in human beings. There is an enormous will to be free, and human beings can endure and resist under the most difficult circumstances. That is a very hopeful truth.

There are two corollaries to this point. One is that poor people are not dumb. It has been fashionable to assume that poor people, particularly in developing nations, are willing to sacrifice the freedoms of the human spirit so long as their basic material needs are met. This idea has been propagated by people who were born free and who themselves would call the ACLU if their Sunday *New York Times* was not delivered on time. Yet they imagine that *campesinos* in Nicaragua can be quite content to live without the right to speak or to listen to free radio broadcasts, or go to the church they prefer, or farm the way they want to -- so long as they live under a state that tells them it will give them literacy training and health clinics. (Leave aside that it did neither very well.) The truth is that even the humblest *campesino* wants to be free.

The second corollary is that the conventional wisdom about the struggle for democracy is almost always wrong. If we had listened to the conventional wisdom, we would never have fought for elections in

Haiti, because all the smart people told us that the army would not respect the process, and the people would be too afraid. But we didn't accept the conventional wisdom, and the Haitian people just conducted their first free and fair election in their two hundred year history as a republic.

The final corollary is that there is an enormous capacity in people to change. Former Communists rejected Communism. Former guerrillas have rejected revolutionary violence. So we always need to keep in mind the capacity of individuals to change. Nations can change because individuals change.

A second broad observation I would make is that words matter. I remember when the debate occurred over the Helsinki Accords. Opponents of the Helsinki Accords argued that they represented a gift to the Soviet Union and the Eastern Bloc, because the treaty would declare the rights of free emigration, freedom of information and the rest, but those rights would never in practice be respected. By committing themselves on paper to those rights, the Soviets would gain a cloak of respectability and legitimize their political control over Eastern Europe.

But the opposite turned out to be the truth. Our efforts in fact helped to validate and promote the idea of democracy. We forced our enemies to adopt the language of democracy even when they didn't mean it, and those words and those ideas had enormous power. When your enemies begin to use your words, they begin to lose the battle. When the Sandinstas began to talk about free elections, they began to lose the battle. When the guerrillas in El Salvador began to talk about re-entering the democratic system, the war began to end.

The same is true about the Arias plan. Some people who supported the Nicaraguan resistance thought the Arias plan was inimical to our hopes for democracy, but the ideas contained in that document about a democratic Central America were a powerful weapon in the struggle for democratic change.

This leads me to a third observation: the debate about which is the preferable means to advance our interest -- the use of power or the use of diplomacy -- is often a false debate. Power and diplomacy are synergistic; they're not antithetical.

When the Nicaraguan elections were over, a debate broke out over whose policy was vindicated: those who supported arming the resistance or those who opposed the resistance and supported the Arias plan? The truth is that both policies made a difference. The resistance forced the Sandinistas to accept democracy and elections in order to get our Congress to stop providing arms for the contras. But the Arias plan also worked: elections that the Sandinistas thought would confer on them international legitimacy wound up sending them into retirement, even though they took most of their people's wealth with them when they left.

Fourth, I would echo what both James LeMoyne and Paul Berman said about the importance of elections in Central America. We've seen that elections not only create democracy, but also end civil wars. They provide a powerful mechanism for bringing the international community together in an organized way to end regional conflicts. A fundamental aspect of the success of the elections in Nicaragua and El Salvador has been the presence of international observers. More than anything else, the observers give people hope, and help them conquer their fears.

A fifth observation is that after the triumph, the hard work begins. I saw a picture on the front page of today's *Washington Post* of German Chancellor

Helmut Kohl being jeered by citizens of what used to be East Germany. It is very exhilarating to be a part of something like the electoral victory of the Nicaraguan people or the collapse of the Berlin Wall. But Penn Kemble was right when he said that we have great difficulty comprehending the political, civic, economic and moral devastation left in these countries, and that we need to be more serious about the follow-up than we have been.

Sixth, that work of following up requires a whole new set of skills and tools that we have only begun to develop. Penn was correct when he said that free markets and strong markets also need strong states. They also need strong civil societies, and they do not have them. We need to find new tools and resources to help the new democrats to develop functioning parliaments, judiciaries, bar associations, legal systems and human rights organizations. The budget of the National Endowment for Democracy is probably the best single expenditure of federal dollars we make in this town.

Seventh, to advance democracy we also need to understand the role of the international financial institutions: the World Bank, the IMF and regional institutions such as the Inter-American Development Bank. We need to understand debt and stabilization programs. We especially need to understand how economic reform and restructuring can be carried out in ways that serve the interests of the poor and win their political support.

The truth is that, contrary to the image, market-oriented economic restructuring and a reduction of the role of the state fundamentally serve the interests of ordinary people. In Latin America, poor and working people are shut out of the great mercantilist systems that have been erected in the name of the free market. But we need to find the appropriate means to help new democratic governments restructure their economies, while maintaining a social and political consensus for economic reform.

The eighth point is one that other speakers have made: the importance of staying the course. We have many virtues as a people, but patience is not always one of them. The war in the Gulf was an enormous triumph, but the work of democracy is not going to be short, quick, and easy.

Finally, the question sometimes raised about whether the U.S. should play a large role in the movement toward democracy, or avoid such dangerous Wilsonian delusions is really the wrong question. The U.S. will play a fundamental role in this struggle, whether we want to or not. The only question is whether we will play that role badly, or play it well. It is reminiscent of the line from a Harlan County song that was taken up by the civil rights movement: "There are no neutrals there." There are no neutrals among nations in the fight for democracy. The rest of the world looks to the United States for leadership in the struggle for democracy. If we abdicate that role by turning inward, our silence and abdication will undermine the struggle for democracy. Conversely, what we say and do can profoundly strengthen the possibility of change and the hopes of people struggling for political freedom.

Discussion

ROBERT LEIKEN: For our first comment, we will hear from Carl Gershman, President of the National Endowment for Democracy.

CARL GERSHMAN: I have one comment, prompted both by Charles Krauthammer and others in the discussion. Probably the central intellectual issue that we are grappling with right now at the Endowment is whether or not a new alternative will emerge to the democratic idea. It has become the conventional wisdom to assume that democracy now is the only legitimating ideology for a government or social system. In the past, both Communism and Fascism were able to serve that function, but now there is only democracy. What, if anything, will emerge next as the legitimating alternative to democracy?

We used to think of the international scene in terms of the First, Second, and Third Worlds. What's happened is that the Second World -- the Communist World -- has virtually dropped out. There used to be a kind of an amalgam between the Second and Third Worlds: both expressed a deep hostility to Western culture and Western democracy. The Second World tried to exploit the Third World's opposition to the West, and the Third World tried to appropriate the ideas of socialism and statism from the Second. But there was also an independent ideological current in the Third World which seems to continue to exist independent of the collapse of Communism. What Charles Krauthammer said helped to crystalize my thinking about the form it might take, and how it might develop into an alternative or competing ideology of legitimation.

We in the West believe that legitimacy comes through democratic politics, individual rights, legal systems, and so forth. But among some in the Third World, legitimacy is shaped more by race and culture. In this thinking, there is a racial and cultural clash in the world which takes on both geographic and economic overtones.

Charles Krauthammer explained that the new weapons of mass destruction will give a lethal quality to certain divisions which are going to persist in the world; he talked about the "crazy states." But as the world moves forward we may also discover another division, one that is a new variant of the old First World-Third World split. A two-tiered world could emerge, divided into those who succeeded in making the democratic revolution -- who were able to modernize politically as well as economically -- and those who failed to do so. Those societies of the world that fail to master the new democratic system will be characterized not only by extreme poverty, but by extreme frustration, extreme hostility, rage, nihilism, even terrorism. Now if you superimpose on top of this Charles Krauthammer's concern about the future availability of weapons of mass destruction, you have a dangerous world to live in.

A kind of ideological outlook can develop on the part of those who conceive of the so-called capitalist world as an antagonist to a Third World that is organized around concepts of race and culture. This new ideology might even bear some similarity to the concepts put forward in 1920 by Mussolini and the Fascist movement, in which there was great emphasis on nationalism, and hostility to individualism and democracy.

Just as, in an earlier period, Communist ideas achieved a resonance in our own country's politics, so the new tendency I am describing could have a resonance in the United States. The two issues that this meeting is addressing are the international democratic movement on the one hand, and the problem of so-called multiculturalism on the other. The latter has been described as an ideology that exalts ethnicity at the expense of universal democratic principles -- an ideology that could contribute to a breakdown in the American idea of a common citizenship.

Perhaps what we are seeing is a domestic variant of what is really an international phenomenon. I mean, the view that political legitimacy develops out of categories such as race and gender, not out of values which are universal. Is it possible that in the future this could jell, as seems to be the case in certain segments of the polity here, as an alternative to the democratic world view? If so, we should begin to develop the means to counter this new ideology. Just as Communism appropriated symbols which were difficult to counter -- symbols of equality, of justice -- so, by identifying with categories of people who feel excluded or oppressed, can this.

I suggest that we think not in terms of First World and Third World but rather in terms of one world, where diverse peoples aspire to become part of the democratic revolution. This would include peoples throughout Africa, where democratic movements are growing, and in the Middle East as well. (As Jim LeMoyne reminded us, a debate on democracy is getting underway there too.)

The relevance of democracy to the Third World was underlined a couple of weeks ago in connection with a meeting in the Ivory Coast of African and American black leaders. Some Africans complained that their own democratic struggles receive little sympathy or support here. So, in an interesting way, the idea of democracy here at home may be reinforced by peoples abroad who believe that there is a single culture of democracy -- one that transcends racial identities and divisions.

Hopefully, what will grow out of the interaction between the international democratic movement and the debate here in the U.S. is a concept of one world based on democratic values. This concept, to be sure, will be multicultural. But it will stand opposed to those who see the world as inevitably torn by deep ethnic and national divisions, where the frustrations that grow out of the failure to moderize economically and politically express themselves in the form of racial conflict and national exclusiveness. These frustrations could take on a lethal character, not just in the Third World, but, as we are seeing, in Eastern Europe as well. To the degree that such exclusiveness is justified through an ideological alternative to democracy, it will have to be opposed and *exposed* in the future -- in the same way Communism was in the past.

ROBERT LEIKEN: Our thanks to Carl, and all our panelists. Questions and comments?

MARY ANN RIKKEN: I'm worried to hear so much talk about the collapse of Communism and the Soviet Union. From the point of view of many millions of people in the Baltic states and elsewhere, the struggle to achieve self-determination and democracy still has a very long way to go.

JOEL FREEDMAN: It is worth remembering that, as important as the ideas of freedom and democracy have been, it took a group of workers and their unions to give these ideas a physical body. I wonder how the American foreign policy establishment will respond to the pro-democracy ideas that are being aired here? When Tom Kahn of the AFL-CIO first met with Lech Walesa in Italy after Solidarity first became legal, Walesa's first question was, "What about the Sonnenfeldt Doctrine?" He was referring to those here in the U.S. who held that history had stopped in Eastern Europe and the Soviet Union long before Francis Fukiyama announced history's death. An American Secretary of State even came to the AFL-CIO to tell us how unhappy he was about our help to Solidarity. "You're in over your heads," he told us.

PENN KEMBLE: There appears to be a polarization developing between those advocating a multilateralist approach under international law, and those advocating unilateral U.S. actions. There may yet be a third strategy to be considered if we are to take the lead in moving the world toward greater democracy. We could try to develop a coalition among democratic states and peoples in support of policies that we believe to be in our common interests. There are structures like the Security Council of the U.N. in which non-democracies, such as China and the Soviet Union, hold a veto. There are many states represented in our multilateral organizations which even now are not really sovereign states, but achieved their standing through extortion during the Cold War. Couldn't

we gain moral and political legitimacy for many of
the things the United States feels need to be done by
appealing to the democratic sectors of the world to
build consensus and authority for what we want to
do? This would not oblige us to accept the multilateral regime in its currently flawed condition, or to
accept as the alternative a strictly go-it-alone approach.

ROBERT LEIKEN: You are talking about democratic multilateralism, which was the idea of the Esqui-
pulas Accords.

RONALD RADOSH: Bernie Aronson made some
very valid points about poor people and their interest
in democracy. Why is it that so many in the American media do not see this point?   Just a few weeks
ago "Sixty Minutes" broadcast a report on Cuba, and
followed it the next week with a report on Honduras.
They essentially gave Fidel Castro credit for fulfilling
basic human rights in Cuba. But when they got to
Honduras, Mike Wallace belittled the whole idea of
democracy; he argued that peasants and *campesinos*
only need food and jobs, and democracy is irrelevant.
    But the problem is deeper than the media. For-
mer President Jimmy Carter just made an incredible
statement about China, in which he argued that we
should develop closer relations with the present
government because it is looking out for the real
rights of the people: economic and social rights, not
the liberties that got people so excited in Tiananmen
Square.

JOSHUA MURAVCHIK: It is a good idea to discuss China, especially after the point about the Bal-
tics. If we take the two situations apart, figuring out
how we should respond becomes less complicated.
For one thing, there are situations where for reasons
of strategy or safety we need to have alignments or
relations with non-democratic governments.   The

classic example was World War II, when we allied with the Soviet Union. Allying with a dictatorial government may be a necessity, and may not pose that big a problem -- except in situations where we are allying with such a government against its own people. But I can't think off-hand of any clear example where our country had some strategic necessity of its own to protect another government against its own population.

There has been some discussion about the importance of an alliance with China to counterbalance Soviet strength. That was a more plausible argument once upon a time, but even then it was flawed, because we always had the power ourselves to deter the Soviet Union, and it is rather pathetic that we felt we may have needed the Chinese to help us. The Chinese in fact needed us. We know now from Soviet sources that the Soviets actually contemplated a nuclear strike against China. The Soviet Union never made such threats toward the United States. A relationship with China appealed to us because we wanted to feel better during a nervous moment in our national psyche. But today there is not even that justification for it.

This brings us to a second issue: in promoting democracy abroad we ought to have an ethics of consequences, not an ethics of good intentions. The question we ought to be asking ourselves is, What can we do to advance democracy in Country X? We ought not merely to be looking for ways to keep our hands clean by refusing to have anything to do with a government or country that has a dictatorial government. This is a direction our human rights activities sometimes have taken, especially in the Seventies, when we simply cut off aid to a country because it had a dictator, without thinking through what might come next. What's really needed is some assessment of the strength of democratic forces in a specific country, and a careful estimate of the possibility that the situation could actually change for the worse. We were blind to that possibility in the Seventies, when we helped overthrow the Shah and Somoza without recognizing that other dictatorial forces were waiting in the wings that might well be even worse.

Generally speaking, it is much better strategy for us to think about how to help democrats than how to topple dictators. Our focus should be on building up the regime that will follow the fall of the dictatorship. This concern is what today makes the case of the Soviet Union a more complicated case than that of China. In China, as I understand it, there is an evil dictatorship in power, and noble democrats are being oppressed. Clearly, we ought to associate ourselves with the democrats. In the Soviet Union, the situation seems more complicated. The democrats are not in power, and it is possible that toppling the Gorbachev government will not bring them directly into power. This is because there are some very dangerous anti-democratic forces out there waiting in the wings. So I favor a more calculated policy toward the Soviet Union. We might increasingly seek direct relations with the republics, and both support them and strengthen them. If we are to authorize a new round of aid to the Soviet Union, all or most of that aid should be given to the republics. Whatever is given to the central government should be given with conditions that strengthen the democrats against the forces of reaction.

BERNARD ARONSON: The people Ronald Radosh is challenging, who suggest that the poor in underdeveloped countries are somehow satisfied as long as certain material needs are met, would never make the same suggestion with regard to their own children. It's a fundamentally elitist notion, and probably also racist. I don't use that word lightly. They usually say such things about *campesinos* in places like Cuba or Nicaragua, or about poor people in Africa. They would never accept that their children should grow up under a regime like that of Cuba; they would never agree that, because they supposedly get free education and guaranteed health benefits, they should surrender their political rights.

Second, I don't think the question of realism versus idealism in foreign policy is usually posed in a useful way. People in government don't go out every day to practice wooly-headed pro-democratic idealism, then abandon it when the situation calls for hard-nosed power politics. The reality is that your choices fall along a finely-shaded spectrum. As Josh put it, you have to practice the ethics of consequences, not the ethics of good intentions. You have to ask, "What is the best way to effect change in a given country or region?" Is it done by engaging with a given government, even if you may not like its practices, or will you encourage change better by isolating that government? You can't answer the question in the abstract.

There's a certain view that we should always disengage whenever we're dealing with a government that seems to have impure elements within it. That has been one view of Central American policy. But consider two cases: El Salvador and Guatemala. We disengaged from Guatemala in 1977 on human rights grounds, and there had been grave human rights abuses there. But the consequences of our disengagement did not in any way advance human rights in Guatemala. In fact, Guatemala went through one of the bloodiest periods in its modern history. At almost the same time, the United States did engage with another imperfect government -- El Salvador. Today there is hope in El Salvador not just of ending the war, but of opening that society up in ways that were scarcely imaginable.

CHRISTINA SOMMERS: This may seem a bit off the subject, but a number of the panelists talked about what's happening domestically on the campuses: the challenge of "political correctness" and of certain versions of multiculturalism that reject American ideas about democracy and citizenship. I was surprised to read in an article in *The Washington Post* about an exhibit at the Smithsonian right now called "The West as America: Reinterpreting Images of the Frontier, 1820-1920."

Among other things, the catalogue says that Manifest Destiny was comparable to our nation's role in Vietnam. It portrays the experience as an allegory of imperialist conquest, even providing radical feminist interpretations of the phallic character of cavalry rifles. The entire exhibit attacks the romance of the West. Daniel Boorstin, the renowned historian, says it's a "perverse, historically inaccurate, destructive exhibit. No credit to the Smithsonian."

So it seems that, just as the rest of the world is celebrating democracy and certain American traditions, we ourselves seem to be deconstructing, attacking, and debunking. I'm used to this, on the campus, but now I see it's in our museums. How should we respond?

ROBERT LEIKEN: Does anyone want to say anything about the relationship between our cultural passions and our foreign policy?

CARL GERSHMAN: Very briefly, this was precisely my point. Just as Penn Kemble last night was looking for some resonance from the international democratic movement in our own culture, what you are talking about here is precisely the opposite kind of resonance. It tries to draw out of our history symbols which undermine, discredit and delegitimate the American experience. May I suggest that this might contribute to a more global phenomenon, that could offer an alternative to the democratic idea? There is a unifying theme to this discussion. I think you have put your finger precisely on the kind of thing that unifies the opposition to democracy, not only here, but in the world.

PAUL BERMAN: I think everyone should reflect back on a very wise comment made by William Phillips yesterday, and that is that intellectual fashions in American universities come and go rather quickly. It's foolish to see in these ideas a grand global threat, a kind of post-modern deconstruction spreading through universities or museums. Doubtless it will spread further. But instead of being a new wave that's about to sweep the world in alliance with crazy states armed with nuclear weapons, I think it's really just the last foam of an old wave that came from Paris in the middle 1960s. Today, America's Founding Fathers are the new rage of Paris. The new rage will eventually arrive on these shores, and all will be well.

ERIC CHENOWETH: The democratic idea has been widely accepted. What stands in the way now are the problems of institutionalization. There may be bipartisanship in Washington on certain issues, but there is no bipartisanship on the issue of concern to us: the promotion of democracy. Only one major institution in America really gives support to this: the AFL-CIO. But the AFL-CIO just doesn't have the strength to carry the whole burden. I think we have been too generous to the American right in this discussion, even though the criticism of the left is deserved. The right-wing attack on the state and on public institutions is serious and dangerous. This attack is impeding the business of promoting democracy. This attack on the state also, curiously, fits in with Paul Berman's more anarchistic, romantic, Whitmanesque vision of democracy. That's not the spirit I see when I go around Eastern Europe. What I find is what Penn Kemble was speaking about last night: a desperation to build democratic institutions that can stand up against undemocratic institutions. Only democratic institutions can guarantee the Whitmanesque joys of democracy.

ROBERT LEIKEN: I think we're beginning to see some connections among our three panels. The last commentator mentioned the opponents and supporters of public institutions, and what relation that subject has to our foreign policy. We just talked a minute ago about political correctness, and what that may reflect in world affairs.

PATRICK LACEFIELD: It strikes me that some Latin Americans could be forgiven for thinking that past U.S. policies in Guatemala or Chile, for example, have been based upon U.S. national interests, not our concern about democracy. While there may be a consensus here on democracy as an important goal, there is a lack of consensus about whether or not democracy was served by aid to the contras, or by the invasion of Panama. In El Salvador, for example, the U.S. has usually only responded to certain kinds of crises. In 1972 and 1977 Salvadoran democrats came to Washington and could not get anyone to take a picture with them -- something pretty rare around Washington, as I understand. Later, when there was a threat to the regime in El Salvador, the United States did make its presence known, and pushed for reform, for democratic political space. But questions are now being raised by Salvadoran trade unionists and other Salvadoran democrats whether hard-won freedoms aren't going to disappear when the U.S. turns its attention elsewhere. Will the U.S. help to ensure a level playing field for the Salvadoran opposition four years from now, and include our friends in the Democratic Convergence?

ERIC SINGER: Joshua Muravchik and Samuel Huntington have argued that it is in our national interest to promote democracy abroad. But, there's a certain apathy in the wider body politic about all this. I'm wondering if the case could be made better, or differently?

Also, on another note, last night Stephen Solarz suggested that he was not in favor of a *Pax Americana*, simply on practical grounds. Aren't there divisions within our own community on this issue?

JOSHUA MURAVCHIK: The answer to the first question, "Could we make this case better?" is that I have as best I can. The second question -- *Pax Americana* versus collective security -- poses what I regard as a false dichotomy. Collective security is a peculiarly American idea. It can only be accomplished through our success at persuading a number of other countries to take the theoretical, idealistic, and long-term view that is congenial to Americans. The Persian Gulf War was a great American exercise in collective security, but the collectivity consisted of 98 percent U.S. forces, with just two percent from the other countries. Now the two percent was valuable; getting them there was a valuable pedagogical exercise. We ought to continue to aim for creating a regime of collective security. We'll just be fooling ourselves, however, if we don't recognize that any kind of collective security regime is going to require an enormous exertion of American leadership.

ROBERT KUTTNER: My concern is that the relationship between the promotion of democracy abroad and its health at home is not something threatened by a nutty multiculturalism. If you were to take inventory of what's wrong with American democracy, you would have to include everything from declining voter participation, to permanent incumbency, to PAC politics driving out people politics, to the disrepair and attack on the labor movement, to the privatization of all kinds of civic responsibilities. I don't deny that some of the nuttier issues of multiculturalism could lead us toward the kind of fragmentation that we associate with Third World extremism. But I hope that the people who are in the business of exporting American democracy don't end up just exporting our country's capital, and take a broader view of what's wrong with American democracy at home.

DAVID TWERSKY: Apparently the relationship between democracy and peace we are talking about here does not apply in the Middle East. The Administration is apparently very unhappy with the results of democracy in Israel, and also fears the results of democracy in Arab countries.   In fact, speeches by Bush administration figures that suggest the possibility of democracy in the Gulf countries are consistently revised by the National Security Council staff, who complain that any mention of that idea provokes the Saudis to go ballistic.   So in one increasingly important part of the world, the entire framework of this discussion does not apply.

MIKE CHAPMAN: I thought that since Josh Muravchik and Carl Gershman are here in the same room, I might ask this question of either one of them. Josh proposes dramatic increases in the budget for the National Endowment for Democracy as one means for helping promote democracy around the world.   How much do you think they should get, Josh, and, Carl, how much can you absorb? (Laughter and applause.)

JOSHUA MURAVCHIK: I think they should get as much as Carl can absorb.

JAY WINIK: I would say, first, how refreshing it is to be here. Four or five years ago we'd be talking about the threat of the Soviet Union and the consolidation of totalitarianism, and now we're talking about the great challenge of consolidating democracy. But I would like to point out one serious obstacle that stands in our way.   If the democratic revolution fails in Eastern Europe, then the states there will tend to slip into anarchy and chaos. There is a real possibility that conflicts will arise that will undo the progress made toward democracy. So even though the danger of mass violence may settle to a lower level, it could still be with us.

We also need to bear in mind the tension between nationhood and statehood as we contemplate the new world order. At what point do we draw the line between supporting democrats in nations which don't always correlate with states? Isn't this a place where our commitment to democracy and human rights can come into conflict with our commitment to stability and peace?

TOM PARKER: An allied point on the difficulties of democracy: We might have to deal with undemocratic regimes which have come to power through democratic means, especially in the Middle East. The major opposition movements in most countries are fundamentalist: Algeria, Tunisia, Jordan and elsewhere. At least initially, Ayatollah Khomenei was very popular in Iran, and the elections that took place there were relatively free.

DAVE PETERSON: I urge everyone to look at the case of Benin, which has just made a dramatic transition to democracy. Benin is one of the poorest countries in Africa. But the enthusiasm there for democracy belies the argument that poor people don't want democracy, or that there are insurmountable cultural impediments to democracy in sub-Saharan Africa. There are, however, some very real economic needs in such a country that we should not lose sight of.

ROBERT LEIKEN: We have heard a lot of good discussion this morning: theoretical, practical, political, and ideological. Perhaps one sign that we are at a new moment is that this diversity of views and ideas can be displayed in such a civil way. It's an argument for getting together again on a future occasion, and returning to some of the general themes expressed here throughout the rest of the day.

TOWARD A DEMOCRATIC CULTURE

Chairman: Bruce McColm
Fred Siegel, Ben Wattenberg
John Judis, Michael Meyers
Christina Sommers

Bruce McColm

The new moment in America offers the possibility of useful discussion between those who have held differing views on domestic issues. Some ask if the dichotomy between individualists and the proponents of the welfare state may not have grown too extreme. Some ask if we should seek a democratic renewal at home. These questions are reflected in the writings of our panelists today, who are searching for a new type of community and a sense of solidarity now that both the "Me Decade" and the era of the New Left are past.

I hope that we can also take time to consider the powerful impact of our democratic popular culture on trends abroad. I find it unusual that figures such as Ben Wattenberg and Paul Berman are in some agreement about the influence of American culture, arts and music on the democratic revolution in Eastern Europe, for example. What are the obstacles to strengthening the culture of democracy? This morning a number of them were suggested: multicultural-ism, divisions in terms of race, gender, etc. What others are there?

Fred Siegel

Fred Siegel is a member of the faculty of Humanities and Social Sciences at the Cooper Union in New York. His most recent book is Troubled Journey: From Pearl Harbor to Ronald Reagan, *and he is currently at work on a book on the decline of American liberalism. He serves on the Editorial Board of* Dissent, *and writes for many other journals.*

I want to pursue a discussion only hinted at this morning: the decline of public life, the decline of civic participation. These themes are developed in my article entitled "Dependent Individualism."

I think people have a general sense of what I mean by dependent individualism. It's the privatizing of pleasure and the socializing of cost which characterizes a great deal of American public life. The models for it, I think, are fairly obvious. Consider the case of the motorcyclist who claims the right to drive without a helmet as an expression of his personality. But when the motorcycle crashes and he's in the hospital with head injuries, he assumes society will pay the costs. Dependent individualism also characterizes the S&L mess: privatizing profits, socializing losses.

Here is an interesting irony. How is it that over the past twenty-five years, as liberalism as a practical political enterprise has declined dramatically, liberal theory has flourished as never before in the academy? People like Ronald Dworkin, Laurence Tribe, and Stephen Holmes command a great deal of respect in the academy, and attempt to create a post-New Deal liberalism. Meanwhile, liberalism itself, in its practical manifestations, as we can see with the Democrats in Congress, can't even agree to extend unemployment insurance in the midst of a recession. What is the reason for this paradox? I want to try to give an

answer to why this paradox has come about as a way
of explaining dependent individualism.

First, the fall from grace. The liberal fall from
grace came in the Vietnam Era, when American liberals rejected what was known as the Roosevelt for-
mula. That was a mix of domestic reform and foreign policy nationalism -- mild nationalism, to be
sure. That mix of domestic reform and mild foreign
policy nationalism called upon individuals to look
upon each other as members of a common culture,
even if -- within that commonality -- diversity, pluralism, and what came to be known as hyphenated identity were important.

But in the wake of the 1960s all these connections
were sundered. Liberal theory spent the next 20
years trying to stitch together a workable notion of
post-New Deal liberalism.

A great deal of liberal theory has been devoted to
rethinking the basis of the welfare state. The effort is
made to link a radically individualistic civil libertarianism to the idea of a full blown set of social services. The theorists have hoped, if I may put it pro-
vocatively, to mate the Marquis de Sade to a Swedish
social worker. It hasn't produced any offspring. Lifestyle liberalism, which trumpets self-expression as the
supreme virtue, does not fertilize a concern for the
continuing sources of social cohesion.

Many of the thinkers of new post-New Deal liberalism became more libertarian on social and moral
issues than the most ardent Friedmanite. But at the
same time that their liberalism sought to free individuals and minority groups from the curtailments of
custom, it also sought to bind the population closer
together with new and expanded forms of social insurance.

The counterculture referred to by Paul Berman
may have been liberating in Eastern Europe, but the
effects in America were more mixed. We have already forgotten Charles Reich as an embarrassment.
But this former student of Justice Douglas was the

first of many to try to tie together a radical individualism and the expanded welfare state.

Reichian liberalism produced a judicially-driven bureaucratic individualism. On the one hand, it condemned socializing institutions as inherently repressive, whether they were family, synagogue or church. On the other hand, it expected those individuals liberated from time-honored ties to provide for one another materially, a feat manageable only by an expansion of government into a swollen bureaucracy. What happened, in effect, was that government expanded its reach, but its grasp was shortened.

Out of a supposed respect for the rights of different groups, the state withdrew the sergeants of society from the life of the inner city: the policeman, the social worker and the juvenile court were pulled back a considerable distance. With the rights revolution, mental illness and unwed motherhood were simply treated non-judgmentally, as alternative lifestyles.

But the movement for moral neutrality, dubbed "dignity for all" by Dworkin, has had ironic results. The divisions in our society have widened, and separatism has flourished. Having thinned out the common connections among people, liberalism was left with the problem of how to bind the population together for the purpose of expanding social welfare. To do so, it wanted connection without commitment. How did liberal theorists do this? Through a series of conceptual gyrations.

If you read Dworkin (it's not a pleasurable task: changes of definition are frequent, sleights of hand are numerous), you'll discover that in the end he invokes the community as justification for all action. It is the community, he says, that will link together individuals and govern action. But when you look for the tangible character of this community, you will discover that it has no physical presence; it is not embodied in anything. It rests upon sets of assump-

tions that are supposed to have preceded the Constitution. It is hard to locate.

Through ingenious jiggering with rules, liberal
theorists like Stephen Holmes, Dworkin, Tribe and
others thought they could command liberal individualists to care for each others' mutual needs. In theory,
it works. In practice, it exacerbates the free rider
problem, the burden-shifting that is already a problem in the welfare state. Politically, as demonstrated
by liberal political icons from McGovern to Dukakis,
it has been a disaster.

Social insur-
ance makes civil
liberties an econo-
mic issue. Drug
use, for instance,
is defended as a
personal choice, a
psychic   right.
Teen pregnancy is
similarly defend-
ed as a personal
lifestyle   choice.

The costs of drug use, as in the case of babies born
addicted, have to be met by "the community." And if
you live in Brooklyn, where I do, civil liberties are
economic issues. The civil liberties revolution means
that you have to hire private police in my integrated
neighborhood. It means that recreation has to be
private because the public facilities are too dangerous.
It means the use of private transportation. This is in
the city; I'm not talking about wealthy suburbs.
Various kinds of privatization along class lines take
place in day-to-day life.

What this has produced politically is full-fledged
flight by all who can from the communities of liberalism. This flight from the rights revolution will show
up in the 1992 reapportionment. If you look at the
sections of the country where population has grown
most rapidly, you'll find that the places where people

live are the coveted suburbs. These are the places to which people have fled in order to escape the 14th Amendment -- not very pleasant places, where your mailbox has to be painted in a particular color. So we're stuck, in some sense, between unpalatable alternatives.

In theory, however, all goes well. I'll spare you the discussion of Holmes and Dworkin. It puts people to sleep.

The paradox I'm talking about is the fact that the post-New Deal liberals call for the breakdown of all the intermediate loyalties, loyalties of neighborhood, community groups, associations that once buttressed the New Deal. In the name of creating newer and higher rights, a newer and higher consciousness as the basis of the post-New Deal liberalism, breakdown has taken place. They got part of what they asked for. But that breakdown which is producing increased demand for government services has also produced an increased unwillingness on the part of an increasingly disconnected people to pay for these services. People are simply unwilling to pay for strangers' problems.

All this has produced a kind of separatism. People who think that separatism is something confined to black nationalism are sadly mistaken. Anyone who has watched the Florio business in New Jersey will recognize the intense separatism of the suburbs, a kind of upper-middle class libertarianism, where people are willing to pay taxes locally, but in no way want to partake in any statewide social insurance program. "I won't pay for Newark," is a repeated comment.

What this break from a normative conception of politics and the attempt to expand government have produced, is not, as Kevin Phillips assumes, populist resentment. What it has produced is contempt for government. I am struck by this wherever I go -- Chicago, New Jersey, North Carolina. What I have seen almost everywhere I have traveled the past year is contempt for government. Not resentment of government -- contempt. And distance. The contempt that was once there in places like Canarsie, so brilliantly chronicled by Jonathan Reider, has now spread to large parts of the country.

I think there are two possible paths out of this situation. One is the path that has been laid out by the Reagan revolution. Essentially, that is to de-socialize government. What the Reagan deficits have done is to force the cost of government upon people at lower and lower income levels, so that New Yorkers now jokingly talk of Mario Reagan. Rather than reorganize or rethink government in New York, where mental hospitals have one-tenth the population of twenty years ago and budgets three times larger, what Cuomo has done is force the cost of maintaining government services onto the counties, cities and small townships. The theory is that when people can't spread the costs, can't spread the risks, they'll cut government out altogether. Instead of downsizing government, making government more efficient by thinking through the functions of government, Cuomo is simply willing to see large areas of government eliminated.

The second path, the hopeful one that has promise for the new moment, developed in Massachusetts. The bearer of this intent was John Silber: not an ideal political candidate. But Silber attempted to reconnect the normative basis of the welfare state, the notion that government should be an expression of common morality, with a broad concern for inequality, poverty and injustice in America. Other people are now picking this up. I hear it in the recent speeches of Bill Clinton.

This attempt to rejoin a normative conception of politics with government social programs, I suggest, could contribute to our civic renewal.

Ben Wattenberg

Ben Wattenberg, a Senior Fellow at the American Enterprise Institute for Public Policy Research, is a syndicated newspaper columnist, author of many books, and a television and radio commentator. His latest book is The First Universal Nation.

As we have heard, a great contest for democracy is under way. It seems apparent to me that democracy is winning. It seems to me equally apparent that we ought to do everything we can to ensure that victory. And it also seems clear that we, the small "d" democrats, will surely prevail. Whether that takes a year, or a decade or the whole of the next century remains to be seen. But the process is in motion.

Accordingly, we ought to take a look at what the next fight, which is also a simultaneous fight, will be about : what kind of democracy do we want? Democracy is a mansion with many rooms. There is American democracy, European democracy, Jacksonian democracy, Swedish-style democracy. Not very many years ago we had a great debate about something called creeping socialism, a form of democratic politics.

When I was in Eastern Europe about a year ago, many people were talking about the models of democracy they were looking toward, and many were talking about Swedish-style democracy. It is my sense that not very many of the Americans who put up trillions of dollars for the Cold War wanted to promote a series of Swedens. If that is to be the result, it may be a thousand times better than what we had before in Eastern Europe. But it was not the goal of the enterprise.

We're not just interested in democracy: we're interested in American-style democracy.   Just take that phrase, "American democracy": we've been talking primarily about the democracy side, and not much about the American side.   Our conversation has been almost exclusively about politics, with a little economics thrown in.   We might now be wise, accordingly, to look at the other side of American democracy, at the American side.

As we win the democratic battle, that American element may well become more and more important. That American element involves more than just a political science dispute about whether it is better to have a presidential system or a parliamentary system.

Paul Berman eloquently touched on it this morning when he spoke of American individualism as our hallmark.   We reject both class hierarchy and class war; we celebrate upward mobility, liberty, pluralism and individualism.   There is a great body of literature about all this: it is the basis of what is called the American character, the American dream.

It seems to me that it is entirely plausible that what comes next will remind us of an earlier contest. Before the Bolsheviks came on the scene, there was a great argument about the New World versus the Old World.   That was the great driving dynamic of the intellectual contest in the world: was it to be shaped by the ideas of the New World, or the ideas of the Old World?   That is one of the issues that we ought to be paying increased attention to now.

The U.S. is not only winning the political fight, the democratic fight.   We are also winning the cultural fight.   As some of the speakers have pointed out, we never could have won the political fight had we not been winning the cultural fight.   The United States government plays a role in that cultural fight. I am second to none in my admiration for what Radio Free Europe/Radio Liberty, the Voice of America, USIA, Radio Martí, the National Endowment for

Democracy and the rest have done. All are enormously important instruments of American foreign policy and so-called public diplomacy.

But in point of fact, the contest for the culture is carried on in the main in the private sector. If you go back a little, you will recall the phrase "Coca-Colanization." All those red signs sprouted up around the world about Coca-Cola, as if America were inevitable. Some people were for it, some people were against it.

Coca-Cola and hundreds of other products do, in an indirect manner, spread a culture, just as Japanese cars spread a culture, or American pharmaceuticals spread a culture. But they do it in a very indirect

manner. What is crucial today is that we pay closer attention to those instruments which spread a popular culture directly, rather than indirectly. Paul Berman alluded to some of it: movies, television, VCRs and, if you'll excuse the expression, American music. We now also have a 24-hour-a-day global American news network, CNN.

The VCR situation is an interesting metaphor for some things going on around the world. I do some speaking to corporate groups, and they feel that the alleged tragedy of the VCR is a metaphor for how the Japanese are always eating our lunch. The VCR was developed in Massachusetts by an American company. But it was the Japanese who figured out how to make it into a mass consumer product. Ten years later, the number of VCRs has risen from zero to 250 million. That's a lot of millions. So the case is made that Americans don't know how to produce and market products.

But perhaps we ought to step back a bit and try to understand better what has been going on. The video cassette recorder, one of the monumentally important inventions of this century, when you think about it, is just a box with a hole in it. The Japanese make the box and we put the stuff in the hole. And what's going in that hole is American movies, American television, American music. Paul Berman suggested that some of the American popular culture that spread to the Eastern Bloc was a form of the counter-culture of the 1960s. That is certainly one aspect of it. But as you go around the world you will also find Rambo and Clint Eastwood and Arnold Schwarzenegger; you will find the entire gamut, from left to center to right. The star of the first global real-time event, Desert Storm, may have looked like Ed Asner, but his name was Norman Schwarzkopf.

The spread of American popular culture is absolutely mind-boggling. In France today, a country with a great film tradition, 60 percent of the box office receipts from movies come from American movies. It's about 60 percent American movies, 30 percent French, 10 percent all other. I was told that this is quite remarkable, because the rest of Europe sees 80 percent U.S. films. In Italy, it is pushing 85 percent. Television is not far behind. It's a little bit lower because some of the Europeans, led by the French, are trying to put on what they call cultural programs to create balance in prime time.

There is more to come. A Euro-Disney park should open up next year in a suburb outside Paris. They're expecting 20 million visitors in the first year. Some of the French describe it as a "cultural Chernobyl."

The impact of American popular culture is a whole field that deserves closer attention. A producer in Hollywood told me that even some of the allegedly anti-American movies and television shows leave a powerful and favorable impression abroad. The Communist governments in the Soviet Union and Eastern Europe, as the story goes, purposely showed the movie *Blackboard Jungle*. Obviously, it shows that in America the schools are disruptive and there are juvenile delinquents. But people came out of the movie and said, "Isn't that incredible? The teacher changed his clothes every day!"

So for the first time in human history, because of democratization, we have a contest for the culture going on in everyone's living room. You can use that little zapper to zap the French show and put on an American show. You can zap the Italian show and put on a German show. When you look at the numbers, people are voting American.

Some of the foreign producers say they are voting American because we got started first, and we have more money, or it's the English language. Perhaps there is truth in those explanations. But it's also true that people around the world are entranced by what is going on in America, whether they love it or hate it.

Ask yourself a question: suppose you took American capital, American screenwriters, American writers, American video technology, and the American film distribution system, which is all wonderful. Suppose you then went to Germany and announced that *Dallas* wouldn't be on the air anymore. You said, we're going to put out a follow-on prime time show, and call it *Stuttgart*. Ask yourself the question: would *Stuttgart* have legs? Who would watch it?

So something is going on, and it's important. We can talk later about whether this particular variant of American culture is trash or not; and whether it is trashing America or not. But it seems to me that it's happening, it's important, and basically it is good for us.

Then I am led to ask the public policy question: are there ways to encourage this process? We ought to be thinking about this. Of course, culture is essentially a private sphere, and we don't want government directing things.

But, still, there are some matters that should concern us. One is that all trade is not equal. The trade-off between importing television sets and exporting television series is not an equal one, by my lights. The public policy aspect involves doing what is necessary for copyright protection, intellectual property rights, guarantees of royalties, and other matters that they're talking about in GATT discussions. We ought to be looking at promoting unrestricted TV and radio broadcasting, a trump card. We ought to be talking about expanding every conceivable foreign exchange program, particularly university exchange programs.

I understand we have about 350,000 foreign students in America now, and about two million more want to get in. Talk about a contest of the culture! Despite what's going on on some college campuses, we can use our educational system more effectively. We still have some foolish tourist regulations. We're doing better now on immigration.

Beyond those specifics, it seems to me that this is an area of such importance to us that we at least ought to understand better than we do now. Things are in motion; bring them into the policy process. Ideas have consequences.

Paul Berman mentioned the idea of manifest destiny. Of course manifest destiny recalls, as I understand it, a certain ugly period during the late 19th century, in which we threw our weight around a bit rudely. So we need to revise the idea somewhat. I think a good policy slogan ought to have some pizzazz, and ought to fit on a bumper sticker. Mine is: "neo-manifest destinarianism."

We'll probably wind up with some sort of synthesis of the various democratic strains around the world. But we Americans should, with every fiber of our being, try to influence the nature of that cultural synthesis. Our values should be strongly represented.

John Judis

John Judis is Washington Correspondent for In These Times *and a Contributing Editor to* The New Republic. *His books include* William F. Buckley, Jr.: Patron Saint of the Conservatives, *and the forthcoming* Grand Illusion: Critics and Champions of the American Century.

I'm going to expand on an article I wrote about confusion over the left and the right today. I'll talk a little about what the implications of that are, particularly for the left, and the future of the left. I could talk as easily about the right, but I thought it more appropriate today to talk about the left, since what I'll have to say will in that case have an end, not just a beginning and a middle.

In the article I describe a number of cases where today it is simply impossible to define what is really the right and what is really the left. The most obvious and persistent case is the Gorbachev-Yeltsin position. There was a McNeil-Lehrer debate with Stephen Cohen, *The Nation* columnist who is identified on the left and who has become an ironclad, one might say knee-jerk, defender of Gorbachev. He was debating a man from the Heritage Foundation, who was defending Yeltsin as a representative of the left. That's right: the Heritage man was describing Yeltsin as the left, and defending him as the hope of the country. You had the right defending the left and the left defending the right.

I first came across these kinds of anomalies when I wrote about the Japan lobby for *The New*

Republic in 1989.   I was at a conference and overheard the conversation of some Washington policy buffs.   They were discussing my article in *The New Republic*, and they were describing me as a right-winger -- me, the Washington correspondent of *In These Times*.   I was then invited to speak on "Cross-fire" about the same article.   As you know, on "Cross-fire," Michael Kinsley is the left and Pat Buchanan is the right.   Except that I was going to be Pat Buchanan's man, and this Toyota lobbyist was going to be Michael Kinsley's man.   It was a stark encounter with the way in which the old terms don't make sense anymore.

Finally, Ron Radosh is here, so I'll cite him.   You may have seen him described in *The New York Times* in an article about a film as a member of the right-wing.   Now, I've known Ron for quite a while, and his convictions are not that much different from, say, Lane Kirkland's.   But here he was being described as a right-winger.

What is going on?   I contend that we're at a kind of terminological watershed.   The terms themselves, left and right, are based on certain historical models, axioms and premises that no longer pertain.   There simply is no way to define what is *the* left and what is *the* right anymore.

Let us consider the history of these terms, and how they are used today.   I want to make use of an article that Martin Sklar, who is sitting in the back, wrote many years ago for a journal back when we were both working on *Socialist Revolution*.   He was writing about liberty and equality, and I think the article still makes a lot of sense.

The distinctions between left and right go back to the French Revolution.   If you want to make a kind of schematic distinction between left and right in the 19th century, you can look at three different terms or concepts: first, democracy, meaning political demo-cracy; second, equality, meaning equality of condition; and third, liberty, meaning the liberty that is associated with property, or what we might now call self-empowerment. What the left stood for, historically, was the fusion of all three, the possibilities of all three: a society where you could have democracy, liberty and equality.

The first form it took was a kind of petit-bourgeois, or small business, perspective -- the dream of Jefferson or the sans-cullottes in France. Later in the 19th century, that dream allowed for the fusion of democracy, liberty and equality and merged into the socialist tradition. Not simply Marxism, but also utopian socialism, where, through the cooperative or social ownership of property, it would be possible for workers to enjoy liberty, equality and democracy.

The right, on the other hand, was originally identified with liberty, and was far less enthusiastic about equality and democracy. Russell Kirk once described Burke as being a liberal, but not a democrat. Burke favored liberty, but he saw both democracy and equality as threatening to liberty. That was essentially the outlook of the right in the 19th century.

In the 20th century, we reach a kind of divide in terms of the left and the right. (I'm talking about America here, and not about Europe.) The great divide comes in the beginning of the century, at the time of the Russian Revolution, and the triumph of Wilsonian liberalism. What happens is that the left itself in the United States divides into two parts. One part becomes what we now know of as liberal. It stands for equality and democracy, but resigns itself to the widespread differences in wealth that are characteristic of corporate capitalism. In other words, the liberal left resigns itself to capitalism, and to its particular distribution of property.

The left on the other hand -- what we have thought of as the left for the last 30 to 40 years -- maintains the dream of the socialist tradition. But the left projects that dream onto the world stage, seeing a worldwide battle between socialism and capitalism, with the center of socialism first being the Soviet Union. Then the focus shifted to China, Cuba and, most recently, Nicaragua.

The left's socialism becomes informed by, and changes with, the emergence of the New Deal, the Cold War, the civil rights movement and finally, the Vietnam War. Its vision becomes a kind of mirror image of the Cold War/American Century view. It sees the world as inexorably divided between a U.S.-led world capitalism, and a mainly Soviet-led world socialism. Thus, for the left, anything that sustained world socialism or opposed world capitalism was left, and the converse was right. Thus, it becomes possible to say that a person who is critical of the Sandinistas is a right-winger, even though that may not make sense by more rigorous definitions.

By the same token, anything that seems to sustain American nationalism, whether in diplomacy or in economic policy (for instance, certain kinds of trade barriers) is right-wing. The converse, of course, is left-wing.

What's happened now is that the collapse of world socialism has destroyed the basis of the left's vision. What remains is merely a shadow faith, which sees whatever opposes America as good, and whatever supports this country as bad. And I had to confront that in the reaction to the Gulf War. I myself had faith in sanctions. But what disturbed me about the reaction of many in the anti-war community was their knee-jerk rejection of the policy, based simply on the fact that it was America's policy. That was enough.

Now, where can we all go in this ideological quagmire? Obviously, the left can abandon any pretense of a vision and submerge itself within contemporary liberalism. This is the path that many former socialists took after World War II. There's nothing wrong with it; it's a perfectly respectable direction to take.

Or the left can try to seek a new post-Cold War, post-Communist synthesis of liberty, equality and democracy.

Let me say a little, by way of conclusion, about what that might mean. Here I will leap into an abyss.

First, what I would suggest is that, as a reference point, as a way of re-orienting itself toward the 21st century, the American left first look backward: to before World War I, to progressives like Herbert Croly and John Dewey. They were the last people to attempt to create a kind of synthesis of liberty, equality and democracy within the framework of corporate capitalism. They, I think, represent a kind of high point of American political thinking. After that, we go down -- not up.

Secondly, I think that the left has to reclaim from the right the cause of nationalism, not in the form of cheerleading, but rather as an expression of common commitment to the economic revitalization of the country. We need to develop a sense that our economic revitalization is a common problem, not the problem of separate, private, special-interest groups.

Third, I think that the left has to understand that we've now reached a very peculiar point in the economic history of our country, and of world capitalism. Worker participation in management is no longer a utopian dream; it is increasingly becoming a kind of capitalist necessity. Worker-management cooperation has become a key to productivity, rather than a barrier to it. A politics based upon greater worker power, and self-determination, right down to shop-floor decisions, has now become a practical and not merely a utopian exercise.

Finally, I think that the left has to affirm and make viable an understanding of government itself as a public, democratic means by which a people can control its own destiny.   Government is not something that is set off against the economy, or set off against the society.

Will any of this occur?   I'm not sure.   What I can say is that as we look upon the members of the left in the 21st century, it's very likely that we will find the same incongruities that we find today in this room.   As I was coming here, I was thinking that this is a group of people composed, on the one hand, of old friends, and on the other, of people with whom I've been tangling for many years.   Many of you are actually the same people.   And I think that, in the future, this will be typical of the re-shuffling of left and right.

Michael Meyers

Michael Meyers is the Executive Director of the New York Civil Rights Coalition.   He is former Assistant National Director of the NAACP, and the former Assistant to the Chancellor for Higher Education of the State of New Jersey.   He is on the Adjunct Faculty of Mercy College.

The leaders of this conference thought that we're in a period of celebration and euphoria following the Persian Gulf War and the emergence of a New World Order, and that a cynic like myself might have something relevant to contribute to the discussion. For an incurable cynic like myself the invitation to participate in a conference around the theme of a new moment was most welcome, although having a "conversation" with 100 people over lunch is a bit difficult.

If successful, this conversation will indeed lay the basis for a new moment in our effort to determine if we have more in common than just our diversity. I am determined to listen, to hear fresh ideas and perspectives about old rivalries and ways of bridging differences -- these differences include varying definitions of civil rights and of inequality, differences that have become sharp over issues such as affirmative action, and which have all but brought on the death of a once broadly-based civil rights movement.

Part of the explanation for divisiveness is the sharp rise in ethnic chauvinism. In the context of the civil rights movement, this means black nationalism in particular, and its polarizing racial rhetoric. This is the latest campus rage, reinforced, supported, and facilitated by administrators and philanthropists who are confused by the demands of the separatists. The result has been a balkanized academy, with minorities hired to deal with minorities, to run ghetto programs, to rap and to lionize so called black culture. Sometimes these programs and personnel assume grand titles, and are not required or expected to meet rigorous standards in qualifications or in performance. Such hucksterism is not about quotas; it is, instead, a voluntary surrender on the part of the academy to the racist mystique -- the use of racial or ethnic identity as a substitute for critical inquiry, for intellectual discourse. "Study cells" are created where blacks can talk to blacks about "whitey," and measure their big and little achievements in terms of racial chauvinism.

This trend started in the late 1960s and took on cult proportions. Now it is pervasive and fashionable, in part because the guardians of the academy abandoned the core values of the academy in a zeal to accommodate and promote "diversity," just as many are now doing with the enactment of speech codes to protect minorities from "insult" and other forms of speech.

It should come as no surprise that the separatist movement has an anti-intellectual cast. That is the measure of the campaign to affirm one's identity through the rejection of other human beings on the flimsy basis of their skin color. This campus-based movement could not have taken root, however, and certainly would not have succeeded had the traditional civil rights organizations not abandoned the students they helped to bring to the college campuses. It would not have taken hold had the most influential civil rights leaders not abandoned integration and the civil right groups not themselves become moribund. These groups, like the academics, compromised their values and lost their identity and unifying purposes in the backwaters of racial paranoia, the cult of blackness and the trap of defeatism. They knew, for example, that it was not possible through the mere passage of civil rights laws to open housing. The practices of redlining, blockbusting, exclusionary zoning, or preferences for racial steering and selling needed much more than motivated crusaders. It required a strategy that went beyond mere advocacy of civil rights or blasting government for lack of enforcement. It required the active involvement and cooperation of whites to help disestablish the dual housing market.

Litigation as a desegregation strategy became a mere mockery when the courts sniffed the political winds of separatism. So, today, society-wide, our culture and language are polluted by adherence to superstition about color. Ordinary people as well as sociologists and demographers regard communities as "black," "white," and "Hispanic." We posit political and economic policy as if it is the American way to establish and guild racial ghettos. Thus in New York, black nationalism not only extols the virtues of collective economics -- a euphemism for "buy black" -- but also denounces the influx of Korean grocers and organizes boycotts against them. It has now become so terribly fashionable -- not right, but terribly fashionable -- for some activists and politicians, including mayors of big cities, to struggle for equality around concepts of a mosaic -- separate, equal parts, part black, part white, part Hispanic, part Asian. It is apartheid.

For the trained and talented and educated, new opportunities in an expanding range of occupations and technologies have opened and will open up at a faster rate than before. These opportunities will be outside the ghetto. When can civil rights leaders realize this? When will they realize that mere protest will not do the job, any more than being black alone can be enough for true self-esteem and individual security?

Don Avery told me last night of his interview many years ago with Mr. Roy Wilkins, the civil rights leader, now deceased. Mr. Wilkins, said Don Avery, looked distant and troubled; he had just come back from a meeting with the plumbers union, which had promised him ten apprenticeships for black youth. So why was Mr. Wilkins so depressed? "I'm depressed," Mr. Wilkins said, "because I won't be able to find ten young black youth that will want to take them." This is not a story about quotas, but a story to remember to insure that no generation is unprepared and unwilling to take advantage of the opportunities that are opening up.

That is why it is tragic and backward to either maintain or recycle a racially segregated society. And that is why it is insane for our educational institutions to institutionalize stereotypes about race. Our intellectuals so far have failed to move Americans beyond rancorous debate. In some cases, they have joined the clamor of the unintelligent who rail against "quotas," busing, and welfare dependency. Some have given a stage to posturing, sloganeering windbags to exploit raw feeling about race and government waste. Others have given intellectual strength to the "Me Generation." The most persistent and widespread and subtle forms of discrimination remain, and poor and minority people need to be educated in ways that can end the need for remediation and quotas.

Finally, the very divergent political and philosophical trends of our ties require intellectuals and activists to cooperate. A new moment depends on whether we can find common ground to come together, whether, for example, we can use our intellects and our influence, rather than the videotape, to do something effective to curb and end police brutality; whether we can use our intellects to build a consensus for purposeful, principled, honest and effective action to undergird our democratic freedoms and promises of equality at home. We know the real enemies of freedom and democracy. We know them, to quote Roy Wilkins, by the "technical evasions and spurious rationalizations of the witting and unwitting collaborators, inside and outside government."

History denies that this period of rising expectations is a new moment for America. It is rather another moment, like Americans had in 1776, in a spirit of independence, and again in 1787 with the creation of the American constitutional framework, and again in 1863, and in 1954, and in 1964. Let us not pretend that the federal Civil Rights Act of 1964 had a sunset provision. It was crafted to ensure rights which the delicate, discriminatory delineations by the Supreme Court have not reached. In 1991, as in previous years, we cannot classify human beings without understanding the requirements of humanity.

In this regard, it is important that there not be a
failure of the human intellect   In embracing this
moment of euphoria and opportunity, it is fundamentally important that human intelligence be used in a
constructive way; it is almost as important as keeping
cynics like myself hopeful.

Christina Sommers

*Christina Sommers, Associate Professor of Philosophy
at Clark University, is President of the Boston area
chapter of the National Association of Scholars. Dr.
Sommers has written widely on issues of ethics in
daily life, and has recently been a prominent partici-
pant in debate about what is "politically correct."*

I have been somewhat discouraged recently by
articles by Michael Kinsley and Brent Staples in *The
New York Times* which claim that the "political correctness" problem is being exaggerated: that it is just
a movement of conservatives on campus -- a cynical,
power-grabbing ploy. This is so unfair.
The majority of journalists who have gone to campuses and looked carefully at the problem are not
those one normally associates with the far right. I
include Richard Bernstein of *The New York Times*,
John Taylor, Alan Dershowitz, Fred Siegel, Irving
Howe, Eugene Genovese. How can it be that they
have gone to campuses and come back with words
like Orwellian thought-police and left-wing McCar-
thyism? Eugene Genovese even thinks the situation
is so serious that he suggested that professors practice "counter-terrorism." Michael Kinsley should come
to a meeting of our Womens' Studies Program to
judge for himself.
I have always considered myself a moderate Democrat. My own experience began when I planned to

teach a new course called "The Politics of Human Nature," and I listed as required reading such dead white males as Plato, Augustine, Aristotle, etc. I received the form we always fill out when we want to teach a new course -- typically asking what the requirements are, what prerequisites are necessary, how many credits it carries, and so forth. A blander form you cannot imagine. But this time I saw something new. Someone had added a new question, Question Five: "Please explain how you intend to incorporate multiculturalism and diversity into this class."

I wasn't sure how I intended to do that -- in fact, I hadn't intended to do that. So I exchanged notes with our Dean. The Dean apparently thought I was dangerous, and told our Chairman to do something about me. As the controversy grew, I sent around a note to fellow faculty members, asking if they felt Question Five was appropriate. I explained that we had never been asked before about the political or moral content of our courses. I asked what might happen next -- would we incorporate patriotism and values?

Within two days I received the electrifying results. More than half the faculty wrote back to say that they didn't like the question, and they didn't know where it had come from. (We began to discover how so many of these things develop in the administration.) I then wrote another memo suggesting a discussion of all this at our next faculty meeting. I explained that, while we might want to consider some aspects of multiculturalism and feminism in the curriculum, the faculty ought to have a say in it.

This memo was immediately leaked to radical groups on our campus, who then went into action. They excerpted quotes from my memo and denounced me as a racist, sexist, homophobic professor who was mounting an attack on multiculturalism. This was circulated in the cafeteria on an emergency basis. People with bullhorns went into night classes announcing that a sexist professor was challenging feminism and multiculturalism.   There would be a rally the next day at noon.   I got a call from the school newspapers asking me for a statement.   I found out that I was not only racist, anti-feminist, and homophobic, but also anti-semitic -- which, being Jewish, was very surprising.

It is quite a sensation suddenly to learn that a lot of people hate you and are going to rally against you.   It turned out to be a disappointment to the organizers: only a knot of angry radicals showed up.

But the real point is that in my memo I had simply raised a question, I hadn't taken a stand.   I had simply invited the faculty into a discussion.

Our Question Five has been removed; the faculty got together and decided it was too intrusive. The student newspaper came out with a series of editorials on my side.   And there emerged out of the faculty a group of civil libertarians who supported me -- people who had been active in the civil rights movement, and are now in their fifties and sixties. They are my strongest allies.   There simply aren't many conservatives on our campus.   There are rumored to be one or two in our Economics Department, so the battle over the curriculum is being fought out among liberals, civil libertarians and a few conservatives.

Professor Stephen Thernstrom had a similar thing happen to him at Harvard, and said it was a bit like being called a Communist in the Fifties.   No matter how much you plead your innocence, you somehow seem tainted. You become so acutely aware of what you say that you feel ridiculous.

What happened to me, of course, was very mild when compared to what has happened to professors at other campuses. In a way I was victorious; I was elected to the faculty Senate.

But on other campuses things have not turned out at all well. There are non-student informers who keep track of what professors say in class, and report any lapses in correct speech. I read in a recent edition of the Harvard *Salient* that there are now a group of radical feminists called "whistle blowers," who go into classes and blow their whistles if a professor uses what they think to be "non-inclusive language."

In the last few years I have been rebutting some of the more outrageous claims of academic feminism. I have written a variety of articles critical of what I call "gender feminism" -- a very extreme form, and increasingly powerful on the campus. I identify myself as a liberal feminist, a rational feminist, but, unlike the extremists, I will not use my classes to harangue against "patriarchy." For example, you can take a course at the University of Minnesota with Professor Susan McClary where you will learn about the phallic imagery and violence in Beethoven's Ninth Symphony.

When I was protesting our course forms at Clark University we learned some very disturbing things. The assistant provost actually had official documents establishing that our salaries and promotions could be tied to how avidly we promoted diversity and feminism in our classrooms. There was a new course evaluation form on which students evaluated our sensitivity to what were called "diversity issues" and gender issues. They were policing us on what we did about these issues.

I want to leave you with a word of warning. This is more than a passing phase. The personalities involved with it have tenure. They are determined to prevail. It is very serious and deeply disturbing.

Discussion

RACHELLE HOROWITZ: I want to comment on something that both Michael Meyers and Josh Muravchik referred to earlier. There is an interesting analogy between the way both our left and our right are responding to the new democratic movements around the world, and the way they responded to our own civil rights movement.

The right tends to try to do everything on the cheap. It is much cheaper to let a group of black kids sit in a room and rap about culture than it is to do what has to be done to improve the educational system so that black students can be brought up to the level of others. It is cheaper to believe that a free election is all you need to establish democracy, and to leave all the other difficult and costly economic and political problems to take care of themselves.

The left, on the other hand, loves to agitate us with simple slogans, regardless of the consequences. The left agitated about segregation in housing, and got lots of laws passed, but never bothered to notice that the ghettos were actually deteriorating because of economic, not racial, segregation. The left likes to agitate about how bad and corrupt the U.S. is, but whether it is Nicaragua abroad or the ghetto at home, the left does not do the hard, long-term work needed -- especially when it comes to economic problems. So we have these huge rhetorical clashes between right and left, and then both sides walk away. The great victories that have been won in recent years are now threatened because both sides in our politics lack the commitment to pursue fundamental economic and political reform. I said to some friends earlier that I never thought I would live to see the day when Communism was dead, and yet our own politics had become worse. That is what is going on today: neither our left nor our right is willing to struggle with basic economic problems.

MICHAEL MEYERS: I concur with much of that: economic issues are salient. Those on both the left and the right have to face these realities. At the same time, the people, those at the base of any democracy, have to apply themselves more diligently to these economic problems. It will take a lot to educate our children: more competent teachers, less administrative red tape, and more discipline at home -- as well as more resources in the classrooms.

PENN KEMBLE: I think Rachelle may have been addressing this problem: two different things seem to be taking place in the mood of the country. One is an increased recognition that the public sector has a significant role to play, and that our social and service institutions need to be strengthened. The other feeling is that the culture that prevails in the public sector and in the institutions of what we have called the "commonwealth" -- charitable agencies, the universities, the church world, etc. -- is not a culture that people trust. The public does not want to give resources to these institutions because they do not think these institutions are very efficient, and, even more important, they do not believe that the values that prevail in these institutions are consistent with their own values. So in some important respects the debate about the economy is a debate about the culture: the country may acknowledge that resources could be helpful in the public sector, but it doesn't believe that the political system and the government will use the resources in ways that will strengthen our society.

So it is impossible, as some here have suggested, to suppress the debate about culture, and the conflicts and divisions that debate entails, in order to deal with what are called "underlying economic problems." The economic problems that may need to be addressed are not on the public agenda, because, until the debate about the culture is settled, many citizens will not entrust what we call the commonwealth with the authority or money to address these problems.

HENDRICK HERTZBERG: It sounds as if Christina Sommers and her allies at the university have been able to vanquish the forces of political correctness on a regular basis. Does this mean that the alarms that have gone off about this problem have been exaggerated by the political right?

CHRISTINA SOMMERS: No. All that I have been able to do is bring about a temporary setback in a particular institution where these forces really hadn't gotten very far. At other universities it has gone much farther. Many English Departments, for example, have been taken over entirely by people who subscribe to one version or another of radical theory: Marxism, feminism, deconstructionism, radical environmentalism, etc. History departments seem to be about equally divided, as are law schools. Divinity schools have been totally colonized, if Harvard Divinity is any example. A friend who teaches there doesn't think they will ever recover.

The faculties across the country are very different. At our own school we have a number of ACLU people, and they have helped a lot. They may have saved the school. So we have civil libertarian activists versus radicals, and right now it is a stand-off.

The debate that has broken out may have put the multiculturalists on the faculties somewhat on the defensive. But this perspective is more entrenched now in the administrative bureaucracies than it was a year ago, when the spate of articles attacking muticulturalism came out. And in places like Tulane, the new phase of political correctness is just beginning.

So if on the intellectual level the new multiculturalism seems to be facing a challenge, and old-fashioned pluralism is looking good again, on another level thousands and thousands of academic administrators across the country have staked their careers on transforming their schools into essentially therapeutic institutions. These people are going to be around for a long time.

TRACY LEVINE: I am an anthropology student at the University of Maryland, and I have some problems with the discussion. I think many of you are addressing the radical and very liberal approach to multiculturalism. You have every right to question it. But isn't there some middle ground which would allow programs in classrooms where students can learn about all aspects of our culture, as well as about other cultures? What happened during various periods in history to people whose cultures were not in the mainstream?

CHRISTINA SOMMERS: I call myself a feminist. But when I first started looking at feminist theory, as it is taught in the new curricula, I thought I would find at least three or four different varieties, and one or two that I could agree with. But I discovered that, in academic feminism, there is no moderate view. That isn't to say that there aren't women and feminists who hold moderate views; it is simply that they are not represented in this new movement.

I often attend conferences and appeal for a moderate voice. And I ask, can't we develop a liberal, rational feminism? For this, I have been accused of being "logocentric." That means worship of male modes of thought, such as logic and rationality. I have been was accused of being "phallocentric." The feminist hysteria has even permeated the sciences:

one professor argued that it is no accident that there are a lot of rape metaphors used by scientists.

I go to conferences listening to hear my point of view, but I don't often hear it. I am alarmed by that.

EVELYN AVERY: I am the coordinator of Literature Studies at Towson State University, and I sit on the Multicultural Studies Task Force and on the Board of the Multiethnic Studies Society of the United States. I have devoted the last 15 years of my life to teaching and writing in this field. My answer to the student from Maryland is: yes, we can study multi-culturalism in history, literature, or ethnic life. It should be studied. But not as it is now. What we have now should be called "oppression studies," because every ethnic group turns out to be a victim of either American society or capitalist society or some group within our society. I try to approach the study of different groups in this country in a more balanced and scholarly way. I am sad that it is not being done this way.

GEORGE BRADGUES: I am from Boston College, and I have a question for Ms. Sommers. You said this is not a passing phase, that these ideas are deeply entrenched in the universities. You suggest that the way to combat this is for liberals and civil libertarians to get together to defend free speech against the multiculturalists. But isn't there a tendency among liberals and civil libertarians towards relativism, i.e., the belief that there really there is no truth? If there is no truth, why bother fighting for free speech?

CHRISTINA SOMMERS: At this point on the college campuses you can't be too picky about your allies. There simply aren't enough conservatives to stop this force, which is moving at high speed. So we have to forge a coalition.

I am very impressed by the political know-how of the radicals. They are very good at forging coalitions. They really don't like each other, and they are always fighting among themselves: the deconstructionists against the radical feminists, and so forth. But when it comes to the fight with us, they form a united front.

It is very elaborate. They have unleashed workshops at all levels on our campus. Sometimes it is part of the official freshman orientation. (I think Walter Naegle said it well: if there is one word that sums up everything that has gone on since the beginning of the Vietnam War, it is "workshop.") They put out all sorts of leaflets and brochures. They are united and determined. We have to learn how to fight back, and we have to do it through coalitions.

THE CRISIS OF THE COMMONWEALTH: The Future of Our Public Institutions

Chair: Sam Leiken
Robert Kuttner, Joe Klein
Elaine Kamarck, Nancy Mills
Amitai Etzioni, Abigail Thernstrom

Sam Leiken

We call this session the "Crisis of the Commonwealth," by which we mean all those institutions -- government and private -- which serve the common good. These institutions have over the last 30 years been a battleground between left and right. The left has sought to turn these institutions into carriers of its programs and ideology, while the right has sometimes exploited the excesses of the left to justify a minimalist program of dismantling government and indiscriminate tax cuts. Nowhere is the situation worse, I'm afraid, than in public education, an arena of intense ideological warfare.

Throughout this period, our infrastructure, once the pride of the nation, has fallen into disrepair. Between 1945 and 1952, the share of non-military federal spending on infrastrastructure was 6.9 percent. In the 1980s it was 1.2 percent. (No one was surprised when a car literally drove into oblivion off the Connecticut Turnpike a few years back.)

While the elderly are somewhat better off today, our children suffer higher rates of poverty and disease than they did in 1970. The number of Americans without health insurance coverage rose from 30 to 38 percent in the 1980s. As work has become more technical, the public schools, once an avenue of mobility, have become less competitive, not only in relation to Western Europe or Japan, but in relation to Korea as well. Not only has work changed, so too has the work force -- there has been an enormous increase in the numbers of minority workers and women. There has been the permanent underclass. We have problems of homelessness, AIDS and skyrocketing crime and drug abuse rates. All of this demands of us a response.

We are priviledged to have on our panel speakers who are up to the challenge.

Robert Kuttner

Robert Kuttner, is co-editor of The American Prospect, *economics editor of* The New Republic, *and contributing editor to* Business Week. *His latest book is* The End of Laissez Faire.

I would like to commend the organizers of this conference, for not a very long time ago the people here would not have gotten together in the same room. This was certainly our intent at *The American Prospect*, a journal that tries to bring together people who may have some differences, but whose differences it should be possible to bridge.

All my political life I was labeled a wishy-washy liberal. I grew up in a white neighborhood reading *Readers Digest* and being anti-Communist. I have had the odd experience of watching people who were always on my left go sailing past me toward the right. But most of us here have more in common than we often realize.

I looked forward to the end of the Cold War, not just because I thought Communism was a political, economic and moral catastrophe, but because I look forward to repairing alliances with people with whom I think I basically agree. In that sense, I think this conference is mostly heartening -- but also a little disheartening. I am thinking of Charles Krauthammer's speech. The downside of our national security policy is that it is not held accountable for

what it has done to our domestic politics, in which there has been a general vilification of the public sector, and the celebration of anything private. No sooner is the Cold War over than we have another hot war, and now another cultural war. It is startling that, with the right in power, anyone as intelligent and thoughtful as Charles could say that the danger we face comes from the cultural left.

Penn Kemble is right in arguing that if the cultural left has enough power to impeach our public institutions in the eyes of the mass electorate, then that makes our job harder. But if I had to choose between blaming the Smithsonian Institution for our difficulties and blaming the White House, I would choose the White House. If I had to choose between blaming the Duke University English Department and blaming the White House, I would choose the White House.

The ascendency of the political right over the past decade has involved more than just foreign policy. It has led to the proclamation that markets optimize, that markets can do no wrong, and that government can do no right. It has given us the proposition that public institutions tend to be hopelessly corrupt, and, therefore, the only way to contend with interest-group politics in the public sector is to privatize.

Civil society is delicate: it requires a delicate balance between the polity and the market. Civil society requires that the state does not become so powerful that it pervades all public institutions, but also that the market is not so idolized that public institutions and citizenship are damaged. The polity is not identical to the state. But civil society and the state share the same first principle: one person, one vote. The first principle of the market, however, is one dollar, one vote.

There are several political and intellectual fallacies to adopting privatization as a remedy to the failures of government. In the first place, if you privatize public services you may be forced to eliminate the public subsidy of that service. In this case, you have to rely upon a primitive market allocation of resources based on the power of the private purse.

Alternatively, you may be forced to pay private contractors for work done on behalf of the public sector. The difficulty in using such contractors is that the same political processes that can directly corrupt the public sector can also corrupt the contractors being used as surrogates. There is a feedback loop through which the people who benefit from privatization -- contractors, lobbyists, trade associations -- become a force for making government as inefficient as possible. This can become a very big problem when you have deprived the public sector of its basic authority to supervise.

Second, the political right is engaged in a kind of "good cop, bad cop" routine. Very sincere, bleeding- heart conservatives, such as Adam Meyerson or Jack Kemp, really believe that the government does have a pro-active role in helping the virtuous poor (the people who want to help themselves.) They are the good cops. But the generous voucher schemes these good cops promote in the end do not get funded. The bad cops see to that. The choice of whether to use voucher services or direct public provision should really be a debate about means, not ends. The problem is that the people masquerading behind the call for provision by private contractors are often people who don't like government at all. They just don't have the nerve to argue that people should die in the streets for lack of health insurance, so they talk about the virtues of the privitization of health insurance instead.

A third problem is that privatization, ironically, becomes a means by which civil society becomes more fragmented. Wealthy people buy their way out of difficulties: they buy personal security, they buy recreation, they buy education for their children, they buy health, and they cease to be constituents either for a decent society or for competent government. I think the Sixties bore some responsibility for this. I second Fred Siegel's comments in this regard; the legacy of the Sixties is twofold. On the one hand, there was the cry for personal liberation. On the other hand, there was the cry for civic, social and economic uplifting. Guess which one resonated most with the American character? Guess which one withered?

Selling sex, drugs and rock-and-roll to teenagers is about as hard as selling tax cuts to business. So we have been left with a very difficult legacy to overcome. One aspect of it is the division within our own ranks. Another is the trashing of all things public, both fiscally and ideologically.

Of course, there are still some cultural weirdos making our lives more difficult. There are still foreign enemies, although they are not all Communists. But, nevertheless, we now need to turn our attention to domestic affairs, and to resurrect our civil society. This will require not only a renewal of voluntary institutions, but a revival of competent government.

Joe Klein

Joe Klein is political correspondent for New York Magazine *and has won many national awards for his articles on public affairs in* New York, Rolling Stone, Esquire, The Real Paper *and others. He appears on* WKBS-TV *in New York on "Sunday Edition with Jim Jensen," and has published several books.*

Like many of the previous speakers, I often say "I really am a moderate liberal." A least that's the way I feel when I'm on the defensive. When I'm feeling sure of myself, I describe myself as a flaming moderate. Lately, I have been feeling sure of myself, so I'd like to dissasociate myself from all those previous speakers: I think we really are at the beginning of a new moment, especially when it comes to domestic policy and even more so when it comes to urban policy.

If we are lucky enough to have a domestic policy sometime in the future, a key issue will involve the tension between the need for standards and the legacy of standardization. We've heard this conflict in some of the presentations here today.

I'd like to associate myself with everything Fred Siegel said before about the need for standards. You can't really have a civilization without standards. On some level, the battle with the so-called multiculturalists is a battle over whether there can and should be standards of excellence.

On the other hand, you have this legacy of the standardization of government services. It is becoming something of an anachronism. Standardization stems from the time of the industrial era, the time of the assembly line. A centralized system that could produce standardized products with great efficency was what drove the industry of the West. Now we are in the post-industrial era, the information era.

The metaphor has changed from the assembly line to the computer network, which is decentralized and a lot more flexible. Flexibility has replaced efficiency, or at least it's been added onto efficiency, as a value we have to be concerned about. And in listening to what Bob Kuttner said about the need for a public sector, I have a caveat: the public welfare sector that we see bloating around us in cities like New York has as its central organizing principle standardization. The question now is, can we move to a more flexible and less bureaucratic social service system, and still have some standards of excellence that we demand of people?

I have worked both sides of the street on this issue. I caused a lot of trouble during the past few years in New York by asking politicians a simple question, or maybe not so simple a question. It was this: How do we as a society address the 15-year-old mother on welfare? What do we owe her and what can we ask of her in return? Now as you might expect, the politicians were just great. They would talk of how we're not giving her enough of this, and how we're not giving her enough of that -- most of which I pretty much agreed with.

But then I asked about the other side of the question: What can we expect of her in return? If we give her prenatal care, can we demand that she go to classes and learn the rudiments of being a parent? If we give her welfare, can we demand that she be drug-free? Can we test her? Also, can we ask for the name of her child's father, so that we can ask some responsibility of him as well? This was met usually with stammering, even shock. I remember a conversation with David Dinkins. (For those of you who are really parochial Washingtonians, he's the Mayor of New York.) He accused me of blaming the victim.   You've heard that before.   I said "Wait a second: you're a proud father, you have a daughter. When she was fifteen, did you have rules?"

He said, "Oh, sure."

I said, "When she'd stay out late, did you ever punish her?" He said, "Not just for being a couple of hours late."

"What if she stayed out all night?"

He said, "Well, she never did that."

I said, "What if she did?   What would you have done?   You're a con- cerned father?"

He said, "I might have whupped her.   I would have done something.   I might have docked her allowance."

And I asked him, "Don't you think we owe these children the same degree of concern?   Being a good parent, doesn't it involve more than just nurturing? Doesn't it involve setting parameters?"

He nodded his head.   He said, "Well, that's a question for the sociologists and psychologists to decide."

That is about as good as it's gotten with liberal politicians.   Conservatives, of course, immediately agree with everything.   And then I ask, "What do you do when she tests positive for cocaine?"   And the conservative will say, "You take the baby away."

"Where do you put the baby?"

Well, they haven't really thought about that, but they might say "orphanages," because it sounds kind of draconian.   Then I'll say, "But how are you going to pay for this?   Isn't that going to be expensive?" That part of the equation is something they haven't begun to think about.

So I was despairing that nobody was really thinking about these questions at all. Until one day I got a call from someone I once described as a "source" who has the same gene pool as the governor.

Andrew Cuomo runs a program called Help for the Homeless, and, as we all know, "homeless" is a euphemism for a lot of different things. Andrew Cuomo's homeless program is one that addresses the nexus problem of the underclass: unwed mothers and their children. He told me to come out to see what he's doing.

Andrew Cuomo started with one model program in Brooklyn, expanded it to the Bronx, and then to three or four sites in Westchester and upstate. Now he has programs on Long Island and several more sites in Brooklyn.

He says to me, "You've got to see what I give them. For less than the cost of a welfare hotel they get a nice clean room in a secure setting. We have very tight security. They get social workers, health care, legal assistance if they need it, and job counseling."

I said, "Well, what do you ask of them in return?"

"Oh," he said, "you want to know about the rules. I've got a five-page booklet of rules: no drugs, no guns, everybody signs in or out, everybody's guest is signed in or out, there's a curfew and children go to school everyday. You also have to see the social worker who is provided for you, and your children have to have medical checkups." And so on and so forth.

Then he took me out to see some of these places, which were spectacular.

"Wait a second," I said. "What happens if someone breaks the rules?"

He says, "They're out of here in seven seconds flat."

"Wait a second," I said, "you couldn't do that in a government program."

He said, "You're right; nobody in government should be doing this kind of stuff. Government should just be providing the money, and monitoring places like this."

So because of all the regulations and the civil liberties revolution that Fred Siegel talked about so well, government can't impose the standards that Andrew Cuomo can. One of the legacies of the standardization that we find in the welfare state is an inability to impose standards of any sort, which is one of the reasons the welfare state is failing.

Andrew Cuomo should be forgiven his enthusiasms. I'm sure everybody who works in domestic policy, education and welfare often comes across these extensely wired individuals who manage against all odds to get a program that is creative -- in some cases revolutionary -- off the ground. Almost always, this takes place outside the goverment. But sometimes you find guerrillas in the government, too. When I talked to Cuomo about this he said, "People like Jack Kemp and Jim Pinkerton, who use this word 'empowerment' -- they're conservatives."

And I asked him, "What's the difference between what you're doing and what they're doing?" He didn't have a good answer for that.

What I think the answer is that there is a new movement that isn't just conservative but also exists on a liberal side. David Osborne, a Fellow at the Progressive Policy Institute, is working on a book called *Reinventing Government*. He has been doing some very creative and sophisticated thinking; more than that being done by those who concentrate on privatization, or the decentralization of government functions. It may be that there will be real benefits to be gained from applying market principles in the areas of altruism. There may be something to the notion that command altruism cannot be more successful than command economies.

I want to say one last thing: I'm not sure where the current debate is actually going to lead, and just how, in practical ways, we can resolve the tension between standards and standardization. We can't have a purely privatized system; there have to be community standards applied to these programs. But there has to be flexibility as well. In New York, the one force that has been in most consistent opposition to the notion of flexibility, creativity and new thinking has been the municipal employees' unions.

This is someting I asked Andrew Cuomo about when he introduced me to a wonderful group of social workers. I asked if he got them from the union, and he said, "Are you kidding?" It wasn't that he paid them any less, or gave fewer benefits; he gave them the same benefits that union social workers get in New York City. But union social workers in New York over the years have managed to dictate their work rules down to the number of cases each one handles. Unions aren't always an obstruction; I think of the brilliant East Harlem Choice Experiment that the United Federation of Teachers helped to launch.

But UFT work-rules now make it nearly impossible to fire a teacher in New York. Two years ago, only one teacher out of 64,000 was fired for cause. Last year the number was four. While all of us have sympathy for the union movement and realize the need to protect workers' salaries and benefits, I think that what we have to think about in this new moment is what role the unions will have in encouraging a more flexible and responsive bureaucracy.

Elaine Kamarck

Elaine Kamarck is a Senior Fellow at the Progessive Policy Institute and a regular columnist for Newsday. *She is the author of "The Politics of Evasion," with William Galston, and of numerous articles on Ameri-*

can politics. She has previously worked at the Democratic National Committee, and on three Democratic presidential campaigns.

The most critical institution in the U.S. is the family, and there are two general ways to discuss its problems today. One way is in regard to economic problems. I am happy to say that in the last few weeks there has been a lot of new activity in the Congress focusing on the economic problems of the family.

The other way to talk about the family is to deal with the educational and psychological consequences of family disintegration. The drug crisis, the education crisis, problems of teen pregnancy, juvenile suicide, crime, educational performance -- all the data lead to one statistically significant fact: all these problems occur more often in children who come from one-parent families than from two-parent families. More and more children are reared in one-parent families, and it is becoming clear that the economic consequences of a parent's absence pale beside the psychological consequences.

Nowhere is this more evident than in the long-standing relationship between crime and one-parent families. This relationship is so strong that when one controls for family configuration and makes a correlation between race and crime or low income and crime, these connections simply disappear. In other words, if you are black and poor and have a father in the house, you are no more likely to become a criminal than anyone else.

The consequences of family disintegration on the perpetuation of poverty have been well documented. Today I would like to address the problem of divorce. This pervasive phenomenon has great effects, especially in the area of education, that are quite independent of economics. One of the famous studies by child psychologist John Guidubaldi showed that the psychological effects of divorce on children per-

sisted over time, even after controlling for income.
His results also indicated that, especially during
school years, boys were less able to cope with divorce
than girls, largely because divorce meant disrupting
the relationship with the father. In sum, children in
households that are orderly and structured do better
than children do who are not. Children need structure, and divorced households are often chaotic.

Another major study by Judith Wallerstein con-
firms these findings. Boys, in particular, have
greater difficulty than girls, and are susceptible to a

 wider range of prob-
lems with school
achievement, peer re-
lationships, control of
aggression, and so
on. These effects
persist over time,
through adolescence
and young adulthood.

Among the pro-
found psychological
effects of divorce is something that teachers and
administrators have known for some time: one of the
major reasons for America's declining educational
achievement is the disintegration of the American
family. Ever since *A Nation At Risk* was published,
and America had to confront the fact that its children
were not learning well, public blame has been direct-
ed at the educational establishment -- teachers, prin-
cipals and school bureaucracies. The first response to
the crisis was to spend more money. In the mid-
1980s, public spending per pupil increased dramatically -- and yet at the end of the decade, we see few
results.

As we begin the new decade, the fashionable response to the crisis in educational achievement is a
frenzy of educational restructuring. I favor educational restructuring, but the fact is that to expect this
to solve educational problems when the root of them

lies with our own disintegrating families is to be disappointed. If we continue to neglect the crisis of the American family, we will fail in our efforts at educational reform -- even while spending much more money.

There is nothing new about the argument that the family is central to educational achievement. Ever since James S. Coleman and his co-authors published their seminal study on this topic nearly a quarter century ago, studies have reinforced one basic fact: what happens in the family is much more important than what happens in school.   Dr. Harold Stevenson studied Asian and American students and found that American first graders began to fall behind their Asian peers by the first month of first grade -- much too early for good or bad teaching, or textbooks, or whatever, to have made much of a difference.

Untangling just what about family structure makes for high or low educational achievement is clearly a difficult task. Obviously, the economics of the family has a great deal to do with achievement: children from poor families do less well than children from non-poor or well-to-do families. Nevertheless, income is clearly not the whole story. If it were, policy studies would be so much easier for us. When studies control for income, significant differences in educational achievement appear between children from single-parent families and children from intact families. Lower income girls from two-parent families score higher on achievement tests than do higher income boys with only one parent. At the very bottom of the achievement scale are low income boys with one parent.

The relationship between family structure and academic achievement yields some fairly dramatic policy consequences. If for whatever reason one-parent families do a poorer job at nurturing good students -- lower income, less time for childrearing, absent father figures -- it is not surprising that student achievement has fallen dramatically during a period when families have been falling apart. In the past decade, schools have introduced many innovations to cope with the problems children bring with them into the classrooms. But, in the end, government will never have the resources or the ability to replace what children lose when they lose supportive families. For example, two commissions -- one in New York and one in California -- found that children with low self-esteem did worse in school. This is not terribly surprising. But the response from the commissions was to propose curricula for enhancing self-esteem.

Anyone who has children knows that self-esteem is a very complicated thing, and develops out of a close relationship between a caregiver and a child. You can't teach self-esteem from a book, or in a class-room. In the end the government cannot raise children: families must raise children. And, in general, the goal of public policy should be to look for ways to help families remain stable, and not simply to provide subsidies. Families do function better when there is a mother and a father. We should help families stay together, rather than devoting ourselves to remedies for the problems that occur after they have fallen apart.

In this regard, here's what government can do:

- Triple the personal income tax exemption for children, to between $6,000 and $7,500 -- the value it had in 1948.

- Create a non-poverty working wage: working families should enjoy an expanded earned income tax credit tied to the number of dependents in the home.

- Reform divorce laws in order to put children first: Mandatory cooling-off periods and counseling should be instituted for parents of minors considering divorce. Support payments should be collected through automatic wage withholding.

- Promote parental responsibility: Hold parents legally responsible for the education and behavior of their children, as is the case in California and Arkansas.

- Make the workplace "family friendly": The President should sign The Family and Medical Leave Act of 1990, which would have established a uniform family leave policy. Where possible, the private sector should provide work-site child care and home-based employment for child-rearing employees.

- Develop alternatives to foster care: Home-based strategies need to be implemented that help parents deal with the stresses of child-rearing before crises erupt.

Nancy Mills

Nancy Mills is a member of the International Executive Board, Service Employees International Union. She is the former Executive Director of SEIU Local 285, a 13,000 member union of public employees and hospital workers; the past Vice President of the Massachusetts AFL-CIO; a former member of the Massachusetts Governor's Commission on Health Care Finance and Delivery Reform and a former member of the Governor's Task Force on Commonwealth Fiscal Reform.

I had the opportunity to pull out *The American Prospect* and read an article on the public sector by Steven Kelman. I was happy to see that he shared so many of my views, and unhappy to see that somebody had said it before I did.

One thing that he said was that liberals spend all their time complaining about the telephone company, while conservatives complain about the Post Office. If that is the case, then most of us seem to be conservative, because we all seem to spend our time complaining about the public sector, and with some good reason. As someone who has toiled in these vineyards, there is a great deal to complain about. What is going on at the municipal, county and state levels is often a disgrace. I hear that we in Massachusetts have it a lot better than other places, and, if that is the case, we are all in real trouble.

I think that nobody knows this better than the workers. Think how stultifying it is to go to work every day, and still to find that what you do for those eight hours a day doesn't make any difference in the lives of neighbors and friends. My experience is in trying to improve the delivery of services in the public sector. I have met some resistance, and I think I have learned some general solutions to very specific problems.

Let me explain one particular incident. Fifteen hundred members of our union are public laborers: they sweep the streets. Our union found that, even under a Democratic administration, more and more of those jobs were being contracted out. Our membership was plummeting. This stirred the union up. Another motivation was that the workers were getting complaints from their friends and neighbors about how bad the sidewalks looked, when these public employees were not the ones doing the work.

So our union did a study. We found that the proportion of work contracted out varied enormously throughout the state depending on the region of the state, who the private contractors knew, and how long they had held contracts.

Then we did a joint labor-management study of comparative costs in public work and private contracting, which generated lots of debate. Much to our surprise we discovered that in every single comparison we made, when government workers did the job in-house it was 52 percent to 75 percent cheaper than the lowest bid of any of the outside contractors.

We thought we were on easy street. We would go to our friendly Democratic legislature and a Democratic administration, and we would get the jobs back into the public sector. Those people were wasting taxpayers' money.

How naive we were! Because what we found out was that no one cared. The whole stir about saving money turned out to be a ruse. To get the work done meant increasing laborers on the state payroll, and the politicians did not want the number of public employees to go up. Perhaps more important, they didn't  want to offend the contributors to their campaigns who were often the owners of private contracting companies. And they didn't want to change a system that gave sons and daughters and nephews of politicians jobs in the summer sweeping the streets.

So, after beating our heads against the wall for quite a while, our union finally realized that the problem was a lot more complicated than just proving that we could do the work more cheaply. We decided to make a major issue out of it. We were somewhat successful, in that we ended up with contract language that says if we can prove that we can do the same quality of work more cost-effectively for the

Massachusetts taxpayer, then we can demand that decisions about who gets the work be given to an impartial arbitrator to decide.

That experience led me to some unusual conclusions about what the barriers to excellence in the public sector really are. I believe that labor is the least of those barriers. Our members are eager to prove themselves, want to have a say in their jobs, and want to be seen as important contributors to society.

When I was serving on the Governor's Commission on Fiscal Reform I tried to ascertain some concrete ways in which liberals and conservatives might be able to unite to improve the public sector. One of the matters we ought to try to work on together has to do with how we do budgeting. No private industry budgets on an annual basis. You can't make decisions about the value of an investment -- be it capital or training or technology -- on an annual basis. At the minimum we ought to be looking at two-year budget cycles. And that will require some real changes in state legislatures.

Second, we should eliminate the civil service system, except at an entry level, to ensure some measure of promotion by merit. Once an employee is into the system we should leave it to union promotional rules and other devices to encourage the quality of work. Civil service is too cumbersome and invites mediocrity.

Third, we need to be innovative, to invite workers to participate in discussions about how they can do their jobs better. Our members determined that if the Department of Public Works could simply invest in mechanical sweepers, in the long run it would be more cost-effective, cheaper, and a better job would get done. There also need to be some incentives for good performance within the public sector. At a minimum, managers in the public sector should get some rewards for innovation.

My last proposal has to do with reinvestment and retraining. One successful example in Massachusetts is the retraining of hospital workers. The hospitals invested one-tenth of one percent of their gross revenues for retraining, because it made sense to retrain hospital workers who were being laid off for other work inside the system. The business community signed on to this strategy, and it is working well.

In sum, what is the challenge in the public sector? From my own personal experience, it is the members of the work force who are the leading voice in improving the quality of their services. Often we as union leaders are slow to catch up. The reason many unions and workers resist changes being made in the name of excellence, is that they are really being made to serve privatization. And privatization and excellence are not the same. Too often, in fact, they are in conflict.

Amitai Etzioni

Amitai Etzioni was the first University Professor at George Washington University and founder and first president of the International Society of the Advancement of Socio-Economics. He is the author of fourteen books, the most recent of which are An Immodest Agenda *and* Capital Corruption. *He is the editor of a new journal,* The Responsive Community.

The new message we need should have at least two qualities: it has to morally correct, and it has to play. I can tell you from my experience that what we call "communitarianism" plays. But, more importantly, I have no doubt that it is morally appropriate.

What is the communitarian message? In every society, there must be a balance between rights and responsibilities. But in the United States we have leaned too far toward a celebration of rights, and not paired them adequately with responsibility for maintaining the common good.

A good expression of the problem came from a member of a TV talk-show audience who shouted out during a discussion of the S&L mess, "Taxpayers should not have to pay for that; government should!"

Today, many young Americans who answer our questionnaires insist upon the right to be tried before a jury of their peers, but absolutely refuse to serve on a jury. We have the common finding that people very much want to cut taxes, but in the same breath  ask that every service the government provides be expanded. Many Americans are proud of what we did in the Gulf, but they don't want to serve in the armed forces. They don't want their children to serve, and they don't even want to pay for the armed forces. This is a corruption of the spirit -- the loss of the elementary moral notion that you can't take without giving.

Where can we go from here? My agenda will be brief. It has at least three parts, and we're just beginning.

We need to worry about the moral upbringing of young people. We can't tell them, "Just say no." That's not good enough. The first moral agent of the society, the first line of defense, is the family. But we have an enormous deficit of parenting in our families. If we were engaged in any other industry -- let's say making shoes -- and half the labor force was taken away, and we tried to make the same number of shoes, with the same quality, and with no major improvements in technology, we would be attempting something very foolish. But that is exactly what we are trying to do in our families.

Let me add that from my point of view women have exactly the same right as men to work outside the household. But men and women have the obligation, if they're going to bring children into the world, to care for them properly. It's more than a question of custodial care. Children need to be educated. Without the presence of parents, it doesn't happen. Our TV sets are not very accomplished educators, especially when it comes to the moral agenda.

One of our biggest problems is that children come to school morally unprepared. Most of the high-level commissions that study our current educational problems start from the wrong footing. They focus only on cognitive skills, and don't appreciate that it is not possible to fill up a vessel that has not been formed. The notion that you can pump more math, more languages, more history into children who do not yet have the capacity to control impulse, defer gratification, or finish a task is really quite foolish. The first assignment of the schools should be to supplement the work of the family in character formation.

After the family comes the community. The largest problem we face here is "me-ism," raised to the level of the group. There are 300,000 interest groups which knock on the doors of these halls of Congress. The sad fact is that most legislation these days goes to the highest bidder. The idea of the public interest has suffered terribly. Ninety percent of government is by interest groups. Even my colleagues at The American Enterprise Institute now recognize that we have lost the concept of public interest. I say we need to restore the concept, the sociological conditions, under which the public interest can function.

Finally, we have to restore some measure of public safety and public health. We need gingerly to redefine rights and responsibilities in both these areas. I will offer one brief illustration: in Inkster, Michigan, drug dealers took over a black neighborhood to the point where children had to sleep on the floors of their houses to avoid the dealers' bullets. Citizens couldn't go on the street at night, and the usual police techniques did not seem to work.

Then a black sheriff came up with an innovative technique. He established a checkpoint at the entrance to the main street of the drug market at the busiest time. It turned out that almost eighty percent of the persons shopping for drugs were not really from the neighborhood. In fact, most of them were white youths from Detroit. The sheriff simply asked all those driving through for two things: a drivers' license, and proof of the ownership of the car. He did not search the car, he did not open the trunk -- he just asked for drivers' licenses and proof of ownership.

Drug dealers, it so happens, don't like to reveal their identities. So within a day the drug market disappeared. But soon the American Civil Liberties Union took the sheriff to court. The case came up on a weekend, the sheriff's checkpoints were ruled an illegal search, and by Monday the drug dealers were back on the streets.

This is why we need to find a better balance between rights and responsibilities. We need to accept sobriety checkpoints for drivers, we need to ask HIV carriers to disclose to their sexual partners that they may carry AIDS. We are not talking about suspending the constitution until the war against drugs is won. We are not talking about shooting drug dealers on sight (as the police chief in Los Angeles once suggested). We are talking about a carefully crafted redefinition of rights and responsibilities to make public safety and public health viable again.

I could give more details, of course. But the basic point is that the country is yearning -- look at any survey, or just go out and talk to people -- the country is yearning for a return to civility, to civic virtue, to social morality.

Abigail Thernstrom

Abigail Thernstrom is an Adjunct Associate Professor and Olin Fellow, School of Education, Boston University. She is the author of Whose Vote Counts: Affirmative Action and Minority Voting Rights. *She and her husband Stephan Thernstrom are currently writing a major study on the problem of race in modern America entitled* One Nation Divisible: Thinking About Race.

I should start out by saying that Diane Ravitch's article from *The American Educator* is really splendid.

Rick Hertzberg asked earlier if the multiculturalist phenomenon hasn't been exaggerated, and if we aren't making too much of it. I don't think so, for three reasons.

First, the Thernstroms have been keeping a tally. There are courses all over the country that are being dropped simply because professors don't think it's worth all the abuse they must endure to continue them. My husband, as many of you know, dropped a course he and Bernard Bailyn were giving on "The Peopling of America" after a period of ugly pressure. The loss is not so much his as it is the students'; it was the only course at the university that covered the topic. Reynolds Farley at the University of Michigan, a leading demographer of race, no longer teaches his basic course because he says it is not worth the difficulties he has to face.

Second, many other subjects are simply not discussed in the academic setting, although they deserve careful study. For example, many Sociology Departments no longer study the black family. Third, universities are engaging in new forms of mandatory indoctrination. Christina Sommers referred to the process of faculty reeducation, which can be quite chilling. There are also mandatory courses to help

DIANE RAVITCH:

On Pluralism and Multiculturalism

A multicultural education is a necessity. The children in our schools come from many different racial and ethnic backgrounds, and some are recent immigrants from Latin America, Africa, Asia, or Europe. This cultural diversity in the classrooms of our nation has created a growing demand for school programs that reduce prejudice and teach children to appreciate others whose race and ethnicity are different from their own. Properly conceived, these multicultural programs enrich students' understanding of history and contribute to their appreciation of American diversity.

But almost any idea carried to its extreme can become ridiculous or destructive. Such is the turn being taken by certain advocates of multicultural education. Pluralistic multiculturalism is now contending with particularistic multiculturalism. The pluralists, like New York City Mayor David Dinkins, say that we are all parts of this nation's "gorgeous mosaic" of racial and ethnic groups; as citizens of the same society, we are all responsible for one another. By contrast, the particularists neglect the bonds of mutuality that exist among people of different groups and encourage children to seek their primary identity in the cultures and homelands of their ancestors.

We are a multicultural people, but also a single nation knitted together by a common set of political and moral values. In the education that we provide to our students, we must reconcile our *pluribus* and our *unum*. We must ensure that education promotes pluralism, not particularisms. That is the kind of multicultural education our schools need.

Adapted from "Diversity and Democracy," by Diane Ravitch in *The American Educator* (the publication of The American Federation of Teachers); Spring, 1990.

freshmen develop ideologically correct positions on questions of race and ethnicity.

We have seen copies of a test that Duke University freshmen are obliged to take after they go through their freshman orientation on race and gender sensitivity. If they don't get the answers right, they have to sit down with a counselor and discuss the attitude problem they have revealed. The questions include things like: "True or False: Men and women are equally nurturing." I couldn't even figure out what the P.C. answer to that was.

JOE KLEIN: What is the P.C. answer?

ABIGAIL THERNSTROM: I don't know -- I'm just thankful I'm not a freshman. Someone said that whatever answer a male gives is the wrong answer.

I should also like to respond to a very important question asked earlier by the University of Maryland student -- a question that is asked by so many students. She commented that blacks also have a right to have *their* culture discussed. Their culture is our culture too. The history of slavery is part of our *common* culture. It's not relevant only to black students. We're in this together.

Turning to the topic at hand, I'm not sure it can be said that we have arrived at a new moment in American education. Perhaps it is true in this sense: we may finally sense the scope of the crisis we face. But just as we are beginning to grasp one set of problems, new threats to public education are arising.

Charles Krauthammer argued that, historically, we have had a notion of common citizenship, and that that idea is now under attack. What he didn't explain is that public schools have historically had a role in creating that sense of common citizenship. How large a role, it is difficult to say. We may not know until we have simply given up on the public school system entirely. But I suspect that it has been significant.

Most current discussion about our problems in education focuses on the teaching of math, science, history and so forth. The emphasis is, as it were, on beating the Japanese. But the task of schools was never simply one of the teaching the three Rs. Scho-ols were supposed to create American citizens, citizens familiar with basic democratic ideals, with the way our system of government and our economy works, citizens who speak and write the common language. So while one aspect of the crisis in American education is the failure of our schools to teach students how to read, write and calculate, another is the failure of the public schools to perform the civic mission they have historically fulfilled.

Two forces are at work in undermining the role of the schools in fostering social and cultural unity. One is the tendency that Christina Sommers noted, the tendency to look at all history, all literature, and sometimes even math and science through the lens of race and ethnicity. I recently came across a chart being used in the Brookline, Massachusetts, school system to educate teachers in racial and ethnic sensitivity. After the name of each ethnic and racial group it lists the characteristics of the group. For example, all whites are described as, in effect, materialistic. All blacks are spiritual. And so forth. It would be difficult to imagine worse racial stereotyping. This sort of thing is not just going on in Brookline; racial sensitivity training has become a big business nationwide.

Public schools are also being robbed of their historic role by policies that we pretend are out of favor, but that in fact are still alive and well. Busing for purposes of racial integration is still being encouraged, although it has created inner city schools with almost no social class mix. Busing has been given new life in Massachusetts in recent years by repackaging involuntary assignments made for purposes of racial balance under the label of "educational choice". This is called "controlled choice" in Massachusetts; that is, choice controlled for purposes of what is called racial equity. Such choice, in my view, is just a more rhetorically acceptable way of putting forward a busing scheme.

As long as there are involuntary assignments to public schools, there will be hardly any social class mix in the schools, for very few middle class families will have their children in our urban school systems. The notion of a common school, therefore, and a common culture, will be in serious jeopardy.

But busing is an old story. There are now new "equity" policies driving families from both urban and suburban school systems. Tracking -- grouping students by levels of competency and achievement -- is under heavy attack. I live in the town of Lexington, an affluent suburban town. Parents are up in arms over the threat to high track classes, which students have to get into to become eligible for Advanced Placement courses. The kids who otherwise would have been in those advanced courses will disappear from the public schools if these courses go; their families have the resources to escape into the private sector. But likewise with the elite magnet schools -- schools like Boston Latin -- which are once again under attack. Get rid of Boston Latin, and anyone who has the $1,800 to go to a parochial school will be out of the Boston public high schools. These will be the last remnants of the middle class in the system.

Too many public school systems are succumbing to these misguided "equity" pressures -- pressures that really have nothing to do with equity, and in fact work in the opposite direction. In part, the public schools are succumbing to these pressures, as Charles Krauthammer has said, because the left has captured the rhetorical high ground. Or, I think, *had* captured it.

I'm struck by the changes now taking place, and I suspect Michael Meyers is too. In resisting the revived notion of deliberately designed all-black, all-male public schools (the Ujamaa school in New York, for instance) opponents have Chief Justice Warren's rhetoric of opposition to separate-but-equal on their side. Opponents can argue against Jim Crow schools; and so forth. I believe we can develop this approach, apply it to public policies, and again capture the moral high ground with the rhetoric of social justice and equity. We've begun to do it, and it's having an effect.

This is not to say that the battle is over -- far from it. But if this battle is not won, then the public school systems in this country are going to be in deep trouble, both in big cities and in suburbia as well. If the public schools can't recapture their role as purveyors of the common culture, if no one but the poor and powerless attend them, if education becomes the expression of ethnic and racial particularism, then there is no justification for the public school system as we have known it. When that happens, vouchers, the use of public money for private and parochial education, will be inevitable, unstoppable, and, indeed, will be justified.

Discussion

RACHELLE HOROWITZ: Joe Klein would be disappointed if I didn't take the microphone first. I know this is not intended to be a debate. But this conference is a good occasion to remember fundamental principles. One of the   fundamental principles of democracy is the right of trade unions to exist. Just as with the workers of *Solidarnosc* or the workers of Chile, the public employees in this country are workers who have a right to freedom of association.

A second bedrock principle is something said by Milovan Djilas in *The Unperfect Society*, one of the books he went to prison for. He argues that what separates democracies from totalitarian systems is that, in a democracy, people have the right to make mistakes.   People have the chance to rectify their mistakes.   Unions sometimes make mistakes.   But such mistakes do not warrant the kind of blanket indictment that Joe just made.

It is worth noting a study that the Rand Corporation made not long ago on the trade union movement. (Trade unions, I might note, give even less money to the Rand Corporation than they do to the Democratic Leadership Council -- so no one can say we bought it.)   The Rand Corporation studied school reform: where it has not worked, and where it has   produced good results.   The Rand Corporation concluded that in those cities with strong teachers' unions there was a better chance of school reform taking place than in those cities which did not have unions. In fact, they picked as some of the most impressive examples of success, cities in which locals of the American Federation of Teachers have had long strikes, and where we have very strong unions -- Pittsburgh; Dade County, Florida; New York City.

There are two reasons for this. In places where teachers feel protected enough to take some risks, when they feel that if they make some mistake they can defend themselves, then they will try something new. Another thing the Rand Corporation concluded is that nobody has a communication network like the union. A Board of Education really doesn't have a means of explaining education issues to teachers that is anywhere near as good as the teachers' own peer network.

JOE KLEIN: I should have made it clearer, Rachelle, that I was talking about all other unions but yours. (Laughter.)

I think the larger question at issue here is a fairly difficult one. There are other choices for us that fall between monopoly public sector services and total privatization. We have to experiment with things like the programs Nancy Mills was talking about, or David Osborne is writing about in his book, *Reinventing Government.* It could be valuable if the public sector were to compete at times aginst the private sector on matters such as road contracts. This happened in the city of Phoenix, where the sanitation department lost work in four of the five sanitation districts, then improved its performance and won them all back. At other times, government agencies can compete against themselves, as happened in the East Harlem Choice Program, which was supported by the teachers union.

But there are many other cases where unions stand in the way of creativity and flexibility. At this moment there are 31 states in deficit, and cities across the country are running huge deficits. But the unions stand in the way of using non-traditional work forces to do some of the jobs unions have always done.

Even if we did have enough money to pay high wages, it might be better, for example, for the tenants to do more of the maintenance in New York City housing projects than the Teamsters Union. It might be better to have architects and structural engineers in training spend one of their four years of apprenticeship as building inspectors than to keep on the hacks who were responsible for the Happyland Social Club fire. There have to be a range of answers; while in many cases unions will have a valuable role to play, in others we will have to scale back.

DAVID KUZNETS: What we're talking about today does provide a common ground for the variety of people here. It is, I believe, the idea of a social contract: what you do for your country, and what your country does for you. Second, what is being said, and I agree wholeheartedly, is that those in the public sector and even in movements for social change have to have a positive attitude about success in this country; they have to a positive attitude about the values of this country. There can't be a kind of adversarialism that goes to the point where union leaders or Democratic Party leaders are seen as people hostile to American ideals.

I would like us to consider whether this new moment shouldn't also involve some new thinking about public sector labor relations. It takes two to tango; it takes two to make the union contract, two to make the social contract.

What this means (for those who are in the labor movement) is that it's time to put aside the kind of ritualistic union-bashing and public employee-bashing which automatically assumes that the unions and public employees are the root of our problems. We not only hear this from Republicans, but also from Democrats. There is a reflex suspicion of public employees that you often encounter among political figures who come into responsibility without knowing a thing about government or the public services -- I think of the people around Mayor John Lindsay in the Sixties. They always announce how they are going to do things a whole different way, and they never ask questions.

These are the people, we need to remember, who helped give us the deinstitutionalization of the mentally disturbed. The idea of shutting down mental hospitals and putting people out on the streets wasn't just an ACLU idea. It got a lot of support from those who automatically assume that anything public employees do is bad, and anything private has to be better.

On the union side, certainly in the public sector, we need an end to the ritualistic class warrior stance. There is still a kind of ritual suspicion in some parts of the left of any talk of cooperation. The time for that attitude in the public sector is certainly way past.

We may need some new form of social contract involving the delivery of public services, where union leaders, as Nancy Mills explained, not only consider how to make their jobs better, but also how to make their services better. This can be helpful, because a lot of problems begin when public officials and public managers act as if they know everything, but are really very poorly informed. (They very often come into public office with very little experience in the area of their specific responsibility.) They need the union's help if they want to make services better.

One way to make the kind of contract that I'm suggesting work is to tell employees that while they may not be assured of jobs doing the same thing at the same rate of pay for the rest of their lives, they can be assured of careers in public service. So if we have to close down a state hospital, as Fred Siegel has explained, we could retrain the workers for jobs at the community mental health center. But there should be an understanding that, in return for a commitment to making service better, a public employee gets long-term job security.

E.J. DIONNE: It clearly is a new moment. People are together here in the same room who haven't been together since they gouged each other's eyes out at the 1972 Democratic Convention. It sounds as though Joe Klein and Nancy Mills could negotiate a union contract that Rachelle Horowitz could agree to.

My question follows something Bob Kuttner said. What amazes me is the extent to which American politics for the last forty years has essentially been a contest between the left and right wings of the upper middle class. If you looked at the typical Goldwater and Reagan enthusiast and the typical McGovern enthusiast, their social characteristics would be almost identical. Sure, the McGovern enthusiast would live in a nice house in Marin County, while the Reagan enthusiast would live in a nice house in Orange County. But the question is: Why is it that people on the left have allowed our politics to be dominated by all these cultural issues? People of the social democratic or moderate left argue against political correctness; people farther left argue for political correctness. If I were a professor who was being harassed, I would no doubt be very worried about this problem. But I don't understand why people who are not supposed to be representing the upper middle class are so obsessed with these questions?

ROBERT KUTTNER: Part of the answer has to do with the breakdown of New Deal institutions that gave us affluent people more avenues of political participation. I also think that the so-called "P.C." story of the past year or so has been driven primarily by centrists and conservatives and civil libertarians who are appalled that the crazed left has risen again, after it was routed from every other fortress. There's some truth to the fact that the nutty left retreated to the university, and it's the one bastion it still holds on to. To some extent this issue has been caricatured, but then, it is all too caricaturable. So, like everything else in this country, the upper middle

class has more influence, speaks with the loudest
voice, and its issues become the issues the media pay
attention to. We all went to the same colleges, we all
read the same journals, we all have the same argu-
ments.   And institutions of lower class participation
have been devastated.

I would also say that we do face demands for
entrance to elite universities by groups who seem to
be asking these elite institution to redress their historical grievances on a group basis, rather than on an
individual basis. This really goes against the grain of
the American tradition of liberal education.   Here a
class issue seems to be sneaking in by the back door,
but in a way that is antithetical to a creative solution
of the problem.

JOE KLEIN: The most brilliant analysis that I've
read recently of these sorts of issues comes in a soon
to be published book called *Why Americans Hate
Politics* by E.J. Dionne.

DAVID JESSUP: On the union question: people
here from the universities might be surprised at the
remarkable transformations that have taken place in
a number of U.S. industries over the past decade in
which unions played a constructive role.   There was
an article in *The Wall Street Journal* about two
months ago comparing the unionized port workers in
Norfolk to those in Baltimore, contrasting how the
style of one union has helped make a port very efficient. In our organization we've been trying to utilize
examples like this in courses we prepare for Latin
American trade unions. And that's an untold story.

On another matter: Bernie Aronson challenged us
earlier to develop some new language with which to
conduct our domestic debate. A distinction has occurred to me that seems important, the distinction
between tolerance and mutual respect. Tolerance,
carried to a certain extreme, has led to a situation of
near paralysis.   Charles Krauthammer has talked

about international isolationism, a kind of evasion of responsibility. Extreme tolerance has led to an evasion of responsibility in domestic affairs. As a counter to this kind of tolerance, we might consider the notion of respect. By the dictionary definition, to respect someone is to hold that person in high regard because he has value. Someone who has value to you is someone you are willing to confront when you think he's wrong. Something that you would tolerate in behavior of the family across the street you might not tolerate in your own family, because you care more about your own family. You are, therefore, willing to put yourself in the uncomfortable position of confronting your own family.

If we try to apply this distinction to welfare, perhaps the tolerant thing to do is just to hand out money. But the respectful thing to do is to help people, and even pressure them, to stand on their own. We have to let people know we value them enough to believe they can accomplish that.

I just visited a very small welfare program in Maryland, a two-year, privately-run program in which single mothers, black and white, are invited to stay for a fixed period. Part of the contract that they accept requires them to plan a new life for themselves, to take courses in family budgeting and parenting, and to fulfill a series of other expectations. The message is that we respect them enough to make them part of this deal. A similar deal might be struck with the people on our campuses who think of themselves simply as victims: we'll help you to gain admission, and give you some special help, but you also have some responsibilities to fulfill. The idea is, we need a little less tolerance and a little more respect.

ROBERT COTTROL: One way moderate liberals might help people build character is through rediscovering the concept of the deserving poor. One of the reasons we have developed an underclass in our cities over the past generation is that we don't reward the people who are playing by the rules: the people who are working, who manage to keep their families together, who stay away from crime, etc. The financial rewards they receive are no better than those received by people who behave in quite opposite ways.

One of the things that definitely should be on our agenda is some kind of income supplement for the working poor. Call it a negative income tax, or whatever: it is one way to reward a poor person who's trying to play by the rules.

NANCY MILLS: One of the generally unknown success stories of the last Congress was the very significant increase in the earned income tax credits. This is an effective income supplement that does exactly what you suggest: it rewards the working poor. The size of the benefit was even tied to family size. So if you're working and you're also supporting your family, you got some help.

This was passed by an unusual coalition of younger Democrats and Republicans. When these people stood back and looked at what had happened, they realized to their surprise that they had just enacted the single largest increase in anti-poverty spending in a decade. The reason that they could do it was that it was built on just the principles you enunciated so well.

STEVE HILLS: The highest proportion of our labor force ever organized by unions was the 33 percent that was achieved during wartime. Perhaps we should therefore turn our attention to other kinds of institutions that can provide a measure of democratization in the work place. I wonder how much support there would be for legislation creating works councils in the private sector and in government? There have been very successful experiments with these in the steel industry: in Columbus, Ohio, for example. In the public sector, works councils in the trash collection field have been extremely successful in increasing the morale of the workers and improving service for the population.

TRACY LEVINE: There are people missing from our history books -- minorities and women. Don't we need historians to write and research what these people did in different times?

ABIGAIL THERNSTROM: There has been a huge change in school textbooks, and, indeed, when the task force in New York State put out its long and really disturbing report on the curriculum in the State of New York, they had no real examples of serious omissions. Look again at the textbooks being used.

ROBERT KUTTNER: As someone who on the farther left would be called a "recovering white male," I certainly remember a time when women were called girls, and the boys ran the show. It's wasn't that long ago. It wouldn't hurt us to be more sensitive or respectful to one another. The pressure to do so can be corrupted and taken to an extreme; undoubtedly, in some quarters it is. But that doesn't make the underlying impulse entirely wrong.

BRIAN ADKINS: In the discussion of Andrew Cuomo's shelters, Joe Klein said that if the homeless people break the rules, "They're out in seven seconds." I don't understand: if the government provides funding for these shelters as some kind of "contracting out," isn't the government still going to be responsible for these people when they get thrown out?

JOE KLEIN: That would make an interesting lawsuit, and, now that Andrew Cuomo's policy has been publicized, they may well face it -- but I sure hope not. It goes back to what was said before about encouraging respect, rather than the patronizing tolerance of recent years.

SAM LEIKEN: This concludes our final panel; thank you for coming. We hope this is a beginning of the conversation, not the end. We ask you join us in thinking about "What next?" How can we harness some of the momentum we've developed here today, and some of the ideas? We are open to all suggestions. These things are best discussed over some refreshments.

Registered Participants

Brian Adkins
University of Maryland

Scott Alexander
Central Europe Institute

Charles Anderson
Executive Assistant, The Bayard Rustin Fund

Robert Andrews
Vice-president, Rockwell International

Stuart Appelbaum
Retail, Wholesale and Department Store Union

Bernard Aronson
Assistant Secretary of State for Inter-American and Caribbean Affairs

John Atlas
National Housing Institute

Don Avery
Professor of History, Harford Community College

Evelyn Avery
Professor of American Literature, Towson State University

Judy Bardacke
American Federation of Teachers

Melanie Berg
Frontlash

Paul Berman
Writer on politics and culture, *The Village Voice*

Charles Bloomstein
Secretary-Treasurer, The Bayard Rustin Fund

William Bodie
Chairman, Manhattan Institute Seminar on International Affairs

Burnie Bond
Office of the President, American Federation of Teachers

George Bradgues
Boston College

Father Robert Brooks
Washington Representative, U.S. Episcopal Conference

Montgomery Brown
Boston College

Charles Brown
Projects Coordinator, Freedom House

Michael Calabrese
AFL-CIO

Frank Calzon
Washington Representative, Freedom House

Bruce Cameron

Marie Louis Caravatti
Georgetown University

Mario Catalano
Young and Rubicam

Mike Chapman
Office of Congressman Dave McCurdy

Eric Chenoweth
Department of International Affairs, American Federation of Teachers

Karin Chenoweth
Freelance Journalist

Marjorie Cohen
Social Democrats, USA

Carol Corillon
Committee on Human Rights, National Academy of Sciences

Robert Cottrol
Rutgers University School of Law

Larry Cotton
Executive Director, Cambridge Forum

David Dean
Director of Research, A. Philip Randolph Institute

E.J. Dionne
Writer, *The Washington Post*

William Doherty
Executive Director, American Institutute for Free Labor Development

David Dorn
Director, Department of International Affairs, American Federation of Teachers

Ervin Duggan
Federal Communications Commission

Jean Bethke Elshtain
Professor of Political Science, Vanderbilt University

Amitai Etzioni
University Professor, George Washington University

Ann Fishman
Democratic National Committee

Rita Freedman*
Executive Director, Social Democrats, USA

Joel Freedman
Bricklayers Union, AFL-CIO

Jesse Friedman
Deputy Director, American Institute for Free Labor Development

Barbara Futterman
Freedom House

Devon Gaffney
Smith Richardson Foundation

William Galston
Professor, University of Maryland School of Public Affairs

Carl Gershman
President, National Endowment for Democracy

Cheryl Graeve
Assistant Director, Frontlash

Robert Green
Senior Vice President, Penn + Shoen

Jim Grossfeld
International Staff, United Mine Workers

John E. Haynes
Historian, Library of Congress

Hendrick Hertzberg
Editor, *The New Republic*

Norman Hill
President, A. Philip Randolph Institute

Velma Hill
Vice-Chairperson, Social Democrats, USA and A. Philip Randolph Institute

Steve Hills
Ohio State University

Rachelle Horowitz
Director, COPE, American Federation of Teachers

Erik Hughes
Social Democrats, USA

David Ifshin
Attorney, Ross and Hardies and former General Counsel, Mondale for President

Gail Ifshin
Institute for Democracy in Vietnam

David Jessup
American Institute for Free Labor Development

Linda Jessup
Parenting Consultant

Fred Jones
Institute on Religion and Democracy

John Joyce
President, Bricklayers Union, AFL-CIO

John Judis
Washington Correspondent, *In These Times*

Robert Kagan
Research Fellow, U.S. Naval War College Foundation

Tom Kahn
Director, International Affairs Department, AFL-CIO

Jonathan Karl
Reporter, *The New Republic*

Elaine Kamarck
Senior Fellow, Progressive Policy Institute

Eugenia Kemble
American Federation of Teachers

Penn Kemble
Senior Associate, Freedom House and Editor, *The Defense Democrat*

Katherine Kersten
Attorney and Founder of the Midwest Coalition for Democracy in Central America

Darren Kinzer
Free Trade Union Institute

Joel Klaverkamp
Executive Director, Frontlash

Joe Klein
Political Correspondent, *New York Magazine*

Morton Kondracke
Senior Editor, *The New Republic*

David Kopilow
AFL-CIO

June Kopilow
Social Democrats, USA

Seymour Kopilow
Social Democrats, USA

Charles Krauthammer
Syndicated Columnist

David Kusnet
Writer and Consultant

Robert Kuttner
Co-Editor, *The American Prospect* and Economics
Editor, *The New Republic*

Patrick Lacefield
Commission for U.S.-Latin American Relations

Charles Lane
General Editor, *Newsweek*

Robert Leiken*
Research Associate, Center for International Affairs,
Harvard University

Sam Leiken*
President, Massachusetts Product Development
Corporation

James LeMoyne
Foreign Correspondent, *The New York Times*

Tracy Levine
University of Maryland

Julienne Lindley

Dessadra Lomax
Minority Affairs Coordinator, Frontlash

Robert Lukefahr
Senior Program Officer, Madison Center for Educational Affairs

Herb Magidson
New York State United Teachers

Will Marshall
President, Progressive Policy Institute

Bruce McColm*
Executive Director, Freedom House

Moira McDaid
Administrative Director, League for Industrial Democracy

Aims McGuiness
The New Republic

Louis Menashe
Professor, Polytechnic Institute of New York

Cord Meyer
Syndicated Columnist

Michael Meyers
Executive Director, New York Civil Rights Coalition

Adam Meyerson
Editor, *Policy Review*

Nancy Mills
International Executive Board, Service Employees International Union

Darlene Moore
Senior Program Associate, National Consumers League

Ron Moore
Communications Director, Frontlash

Steven Morris
Visiting Fellow, Harvard University

Emanuel Muravchik
Social Democrats, USA

Joshua Muravchik
Resident Scholar, American Enterprise Institute

Walter Naegle
Executive Director, The Bayard Rustin Fund

Victor Nakas
Director, Lithuanian Information Center

Victoria Nuland
Soviet Desk, U.S. Department of State

Deborah Owens
Retail, Wholesale and Department Store Workers Union

Barabara Pape
American Federation of Teachers

Tom Parker
Office of Senator Joseph Lieberman

Douglas Payne
Director of Hemispheric Studies, Freedom House

Ruth Perlmutter
Sociologist

Martin Peretz
Editor-in-Chief, *The New Republic*

Dave Peterson
National Endowment for Democracy

John Philip
Student, Columbia University Law School

William Phillips
Editor-in-Chief, *Partisan Review*

Marc Plattner
Co-Editor, *Journal of Democracy*

Ronald Radosh*
Professor of History, City University of New York

Diane Ravitch
Adjunct Professor of History and Education, Teachers College, Columbia University

Walter Raymond
Deputy Director, U.S. Information Agency

Otto J. Reich
The Brock Group; formerly U.S. Ambassador to Venezuela

Mary Ann Rikken
Estonian-American National Council

Aaron Rhodes
Boston University and Institut fur die Wissenschaften vom Menshcen, Vienna

Bella Rosenberg
Assistant to the President, American Federation of Teachers

Wendy Sawitz
Social Democrats, USA

Yetta Schactman
Social Democrats, USA

Simon Serfaty
Foreign Policy Institute, Johns Hopkins School of Advanced International Studies

Don Shannon
Washington Correspondent, Los Angeles Times

Sally Shannon

Nina Shea
President, Puebla Institute

Ambassador Sally Shelton
Georgetown University

Fred Siegel
Professor of History and Humanities, The Cooper Union

Eric Singer
Research Associate, Freedom House

Martin Sklar
Professor of History, Bucknell University

Don Slaiman
League for Industrial Democracy

Jessica Smith
Seafarers International Union

Nelson Smith
Director of Programs for the Improvement of Practice, U.S. Department of Education

Congressman Stephen Solarz (D-NY)

Christina Sommers
Professor of Philosophy, Clark University

Thomas Spragens, Jr.
Professor of Political Science, Duke University

Sol Stern

Joan Suall
Social Democrats, USA

Sandor Szilagyi
Writer and Filmmaker (Hungary)

David Tappin
Boston College

Mary Temple
Executive Director, Curry Foundation

Abigail Thernstrom
Olin Fellow, Boston University School of Education

Stephan Thernstrom
Professor of History, Harvard University

Victoria Thomas
Freedom House

Jackson Toby
Professor of Sociology, Rutgers University

Miro Todorovich
Universities Center for Rational Alternatives

Helen Toth
Special Assistant, American Postal Workers Union

Steve Tullberg
Director, Indian Law Resource Center

David Twersky
Associate Editor, *The Forward*

Jane Usdan
American Federation of Teachers

Michael Verdue
American Institute for Free Labor Development

Ruth Wattenberg
Coordinator, Education for Democracy Project, American
Federation of Teachers

Ben Wattenberg
Senior Fellow, American Enterprise Institute, and
syndicated columnist

Jay Winik
National Defense University

* Panel Chair